EMPOWER YOUR SUCCESS SERIES

BY SCOTT ALLAN

Empower Your
Deep Focus.

Other Books by Scott Allan

For future book releases,
you can follow Scott Allan here:
author.to/ScottAllanBooks

Empower Your Thoughts: Control Worry and Anxiety, Develop a Positive Mental Attitude, and Master Your Mindset

Empower Your Fear: Leverage Your Fears To Rise Above Mediocrity and Turn Self-Doubt Into a Confident Plan of Action

Empower Your Success: Success Strategies to Maximize Performance, Take Positive Action, and Engage Your Enthusiasm for Living a Great Life

Rejection Reset: A Strategic Step-By-Step Program for Restoring Self-Confidence, Reshaping an Inferior Mindset, and Thriving In a Shame-Free Lifestyle

Rejection Free: How to Choose Yourself First and Take Charge of Your Life By Confidently Asking For What You Want

Do It Scared: Charge Forward with Confidence, Conquer Resistance, and Break Through Your Limitations

Relaunch Your Life: Break the Cycle of Self-Defeat, Destroy Negative Emotions, and Reclaim Your Personal Power

Drive Your Destiny: Create a Vision for Your Life, Build Better Habits for Wealth and Health, and Unlock Your Inner Greatness

The Discipline of Masters: Destroy Big Obstacles, Master Your Time, Capture Creative Ideas and Become the Leader You Were Born to Be

The Master of Achievement: Conquer Fear and Adversity, Maximize Big Goals, Supercharge Your Success and Develop a Purpose Driven Mindset

Do the Hard Things First: How to Win Over Procrastination and Master the Habit of Doing Difficult Work

Empower Your
Deep Focus

Win Over Distraction, Master Your Attention, and Train Your Brain to Improve Memory, Concentration, and Cognitive Skills

By Scott Allan

Copyright © 2021 by **Scott Allan Publishing** all rights reserved.

Empower Your Deep Focus by Scott Allan

All rights reserved. No part of this book may be reproduced in any form without permission in writing from the author. Reviewers may quote brief passages in reviews.

While all attempts have been made to verify the information provided in this publication, neither the author nor the publisher assumes any responsibility for errors, omissions, or contrary interpretation of the subject matter herein.

The views expressed in this publication are those of the author alone and should not be taken as expert instruction or commands. The reader is responsible for his or her own actions, as well as his or her own interpretation of the material found within this publication.

Adherence to all applicable laws and regulations, including international, federal, state and local governing professional licensing, business practices, advertising, and all other aspects of doing business in the US, Canada or any other jurisdiction is the sole responsibility of the reader and consumer.

Neither the author nor the publisher assumes any responsibility or liability whatsoever on behalf of the consumer or reader of this material. Any perceived slight of any individual or organization is purely unintentional.

ISBN (Paperback): 978-1-989599-56-3
eISBN: 978-1-989599-55-6
ISBN Hardcover: 978-1-989599-57-0

CONTENTS

Introduction: Elements of Deep Focus 13
Part I: What Deep Focus is, and Why it Matters 21
What is Deep Focus? 23
Why Focus Matters 29
The Different Types of Focus 32
The Process of Building Focus 39
Part II: Eliminate the Obstacles to Focus 45
7 Common Obstacles that Block Focus 47
Part III: 59
The Focus Mindset 59
Controlling the Fear of Failure 61
Consciously Adopting a Positive Mindset 65
Getting into the Focus Zone 69
Part IV: 73
Strategy Execution for Concentration, Flow and Energy 73
19 Strategies to Maximize Deep Focus 75
   Strategy 1: Apply the 2-Minute Rule 78
   Strategy 3: Simplify Your Decision-Making Process 82
   Strategy 4: Improve Your Time Batching 84
   Strategy 5: Use 'halfway' Breaks 87
   Strategy 6: Schedule Your Morning Power Hour 89
   Strategy 7: Prioritize Tasks with the 'ABCDE' Method 91
   Strategy 8: Make a 'things-not-to-do' List 93
   Strategy 9: Use Music to Sharpen Focus 95

Strategy 10: Learn When and How to Say *No*.................................. 97

Strategy 11: Get Offline and Turn Off Your Phone......................... 99

Strategy 12: Connect with an Accountability Partner 101

Strategy 13: Make Easy-to-Reference Notes When You Read 103

Strategy 14: Track Your Small Wins 105

Strategy 15: Set Healthy Boundaries 107

Strategy 16: Create (and Stick to) a Daily Routine.......................... 109

Strategy 17: Get Rid of Your Obsession with Perfection................ 111

Strategy 18: Assess Your Selective Attention................................. 113

Strategy 19: Release Your Past, Visualize Your Future, and Focus on Your Present.. 115

Part V:...117

Feed Your Focus 117

Using 'Focus Fuel' to Feed Deep Focus (and keep going)................119

Empower Your Deep Focus: Conclusion 125

About Scott Allan 128

Bonus: Free Training Guide

As a way of saying thanks for your purchase, I'm offering a free digital product that's exclusive to my readers.

The Fearless Confidence Action Guide: 17 Action Plans for Overcoming Fear and Increasing Confidence

Scan the QR code below to access your copy NOW.

Gain Access to 17 Action Plans Guaranteed to Reinvent the Way You Live Your LIFE… Gail All Access Here and Subscribe to My Newsletter for Weekly Strategies and Tactics for Living an Undefeated Lifestyle!

"If you **design your life** so that you spend most of your time working on things you are **passionate** about and **proficient** at, the **discipline** to do those things comes easily."

— *Michael Hyatt, Free to Focus: A Total Productivity System to Achieve More by Doing Less*

Introduction: Elements of Deep Focus

"Scott? Scott Allan, do you know the answer?"

My attention on the birds in the tree just outside the classroom window had suddenly been broken from a voice bellowing at me from the front of the room. As I turned back to the lesson (what class was this?), I noticed the entire class had diverted its attention to the guy who never paid attention to anything. He was always lost in some mystical daydream, or thinking about something else during class time. That could explain why he had the lowest scores in class.

That guy was me, and as far back as I can remember, focus was always a goal I could never succeed at. I always wanted to be someplace else doing something else with somebody else. But here I was in the third year of University (Yes, this is Uni, not Junior High School) with the professor at the front of the room impatiently staring at me waiting for an answer.

"Well? Do you know or not?"

Apparently—from my dreamy like state—I did not. I could see from the schematic on the board (when had that appeared?) that it had something to do with mathematics. There were a lot of formulas and other symbols I still hadn't wrapped my head around. I responded, as I do with most things that catch me off guard: "Give me a moment to think about it." That became my favorite line I used throughout life that roughly translated, "You're better off asking someone else."

Later in life I would be diagnosed with ADHD which, as you may know, impacts the brain's ability to focus on any one thing for any length of time. But that wasn't my issue. I just had limited interest in many things, including school subjects, small talk, or mindless television shows about happy families or friends that always appeared to have some magical life greater than my own.

In our daily life, we are told to stay focused on work, stay focused on your finances, your goals, and don't get distracted by cat videos or Reels on Instagram. But what if you like cat videos and decide to focus on this as a side business that ends up making you millions of dollars and you build up a fanbase of 200,000 followers?

Was focusing on this a "bad idea?" Hell no, go find some more cats and get creative. What I learned about focus over the years is simply this:

Whatever you focus on, you become. What you focus on makes life happen.

The point is, just because people disapprove of what you focus on doesn't mean you should stop it. I'm not going to suggest you stop spending time on YouTube because "I" think it's a waste of time. What matters is what *you* think and how *you* feel about the time you spend focusing on something.

Are you achieving your goals? Do you have any goals to focus on? What do you fio

Deep Focus is about focusing on what you love to do. If you're sitting in a classroom all day and the subject is of no interest to you at all (as it was for me), I don't care how powerful your mind is, you will direct your thoughts towards something more fun and intoxicating. That's our nature. Forced focus is exhausting and drains your mental battery.

How about those long business meetings you have to sit in and try to look interested in? Or when your partner is telling you about the latest office gossip in the workplace and you have to respond with an overly exaggerated, "Oh my god, she did what?" when all you really want is the conversation to end.

You can pretend to be interested in just about anything but focusing all in is the difference between people who succeed in doing incredible things, and those that don't. Anyone who builds a brand or company, and is highly successful in one field and loves what they do, are so focused on that *one thing* that success becomes inevitable.

Focus works best when you are really present during the work. When you work towards *your* goals and not the goals or KPIs (Key

Performance Indicators) set by another individual or company. You will always be more focused and aligned to perform at a deeper level of focus when it's a project or activity you decide is worth it.

I believe that focus begins with acquiring a deep interest in something. Yes, there are many situations when we must look interested or appear focused, but as long as you recognize when to fake it and when it really matters.

This book will teach you basic strategies for tapping into this level of focus at will. It doesn't matter if your mind has been a slave to distraction. It is time to break the shackles of distraction and deep dive into your flow state.

Who is this book for (and why you need it)?

This book is for you IF you are all over the place with your focus. This is also called distraction or focusing on things that don't matter (which is really the same thing as distraction).

You need Deep Focus if you:

- lose concentration every two minutes

- suddenly find yourself working on a different task with no memory of how you got there.

- Think responding to email all afternoon defines *productivity*.

- Bought another shiny object (Shiny Object Syndrome) and the next day are deeply regretting it.

- Collect so much information that you lose track of everything

- want to be productive and efficient, but at the end of the day, you run out of time and everything on your to do list since last week is still on your to do list.

- You daydream all the time and do nothing else (This could be a positive trait, but not if you're running a company and expected to be present most of the time).

I'm sure you have your own reasons for needing to be a focused machine. But the purpose for this book isn't to turn you into a productivity monster, or help you to "get more done in less time."

Our goal here is to *train your brain* for deep focus for a short amount of time.

Focus—**Deep Focus**—is about managing mental energy—or directing your thoughts into a laser-focused stream—while ignoring the multitude of distractions competing for your attention.

You can get as much work done in two hours as you can in eight. You can shorten your work day, conserve mental power, and have enough left over at the end of your day for fun and relaxation (the rewards of living a deeply focused life).

Focus is not something you are born with but, it is a skill that you train for. Yes, other factors do affect our focus—ADHD, environment, relationships—but the concept is to focus on what you can control.

It's about reshaping your mind to stay fixed on one path until a conclusion (outcome) has been achieved. I'm referring to your goals and dreams. People who accomplish so much in the same amount of time as the rest of humanity have the same amount of time. They just manage their focus and work on one thing that engages their attention until finished.

The Deep Focus Structure (and how to implement this material)

Here is a breakdown of the material in this book. I recommend reading the chapters (and sections) in the order they appear.

Part 1: What is Deep Focus and Why It Matters. You will learn about the **purpose of deep focus** and the **positive impact** it has on building the quality of your life. We will also cover the different types of focus, and the process of building focus for long-term sustainability.

Part 2: Eliminate the Obstacles to Focus. You will learn about the common barriers to focus and how to remove them. You will learn the keys to creating a healthier environment for focus as well as developing a positive attitude toward failure.

Part 3: The Focus Mindset. You will focus on strategies for controlling the fear of failure and how to adopt a positive attitude. This includes a system for getting into the deep state of flow and overcoming Shiny Object Syndrome.

Part 4—the real "guts" of this program—are made up of **19 strategies for deep implementation** that teaches you how to optimize your time and mental clarity for deep focus. You will learn the best tactics for *Deep Focus* that include how to:

- Apply the 2-minute rule
- Begin with small chunks of hyper-focused work
- Make it easier for yourself to make decisions
- Schedule morning power hours
- Prioritize using the 'ABCDE' method
- Use music to sharpen your focus
- Learn when and how to say 'no'
- Track your small wins
- Set healthy boundaries
- Create and stick to a daily routine
- Get rid of your perfection obsession
- Assess your selective attention

Finally, in **Part 5: Feed Your Focus**, you will learn how to use Focus Fuel with the five focus fuel methods that include how to:

- Optimize your focus environment and create your 'focus dome'
- Get enough sleep everyday
- Eat right and begin your day with a healthy meal
- Kick off your day with exercise and energy
- Practice meditation to eliminate worry and anxiety

Now, it's time to begin your deep focus training.

Let's dive in and get to work.

Empower Your Success Series

Additionally, remember to check out the entire **Empower Your Success series** for all available titles. You can actualize all your dreams and goals, take control of your mindset, and govern your thoughts through the systems and in-depth training taught in each book.

As you work through each book in the series, you will be empowered with unbreakable confidence and action-focused strategies designed to get you the results you need.

You can access all available titles in this series here:

<u>Scott Allan's Empower Your Success Series</u>

See you on the inside!

"Successful people maintain a **positive focus** in life no matter what is going on around them. They **stay focused** on their past successes rather than their past **failures**, and on the next action steps they need to take to get them closer to the fulfillment of their **goals** rather than all the other **distractions** that life presents to them."

— **Jack Canfield,** bestselling author of *The Success Principles*

Part I: What Deep Focus is, and Why it Matters

"It is those who concentrate on but one thing at a time who advance in this world."

Og Mandino

What is Deep Focus?

Countless sources, from modern day celebrities and speakers to the ancient texts such as the Bible and the Gita, emphasize on the tenet that what you *focus* on is what grows.

Focus, as defined by Webster's, is 'a point of concentration.' To focus is essentially to channel your attention, energy and actions towards something specific, at the exclusion of other things.

Inherent in the definition of focus, then, is the need to put aside several other things and choose one main thing. Of course, you can get around to your other tasks later, but for a given moment, you need to pick what is most important to you, concentrate on just this one key task or agenda, and say no to absolutely everything else.

There can be **no success without focus**, unless it happens by chance. Two of the most successful men of the 21st century, Bill Gates and Warren Buffett, both cite focus as the single most important ingredient for their success.

To maximize focus, pursue a single task or goal at a time, eliminate your distractions, and ensure an environment that supports concentration.

This is the key to success in anything you are pursuing. People who achieve their dreams—while everyone else is distracted and chasing shiny objects—live happier, healthier lives.

The question you must ask yourself, as you read through this book is, "Will I be a person of deep focus, or allow myself to be influenced by distraction?"

I know you'll make the right choice.

Hyper Focus and Deep Focus – What's the Difference?

Deep focus, the kind of intense focus required to succeed at the highest level in any endeavor, is different from hyper focus. You may have heard of ADHD, or 'Attention deficit hyperactivity disorder;' it is a neurological condition in which some of the brain's ability to plan, focus on, and execute activities is impaired.

ADHD is diagnosed in children and adults alike, and it is a condition that makes people hyperactive, impulsive, inattentive, or all of these. Both, a lack of focus, as well as the other extreme - hyper focus, are often cited as common symptoms of ADHD.

Hyper focus is a condition wherein a person is able to concentrate intensely, but is not able to regulate or direct his or her attention to the desired activity. The person may have a tough time completing mundane tasks, but might happily perform tasks which are of interest to him or her.

For example, a child with ADHD may not be able to complete his homework but may be able to focus for hours on video games. Losing track of time and ignoring one's responsibilities are, as expected, common consequences of ADHD.

It is possible to cope with, manage and even learn to harness hyper focus positively. Being entirely engrossed in something specific, while shutting out the rest of the world, or 'being in the zone' as some people call it, can be a wonderful thing, if used for something productive.

Here's how (and why) we lose focus

Human beings have evolved over hundreds of thousands of years, with some aspects of our minds and bodies getting fine-tuned, others becoming obsolete, and yet others remaining deep-rooted and hard-wired. We are, in a way, programmed to lose focus.

Our ancestors needed to heed to dangerous and threatening stimulants; in many cases it meant life or death. In other words, our brains are wired to see distractions as threats and to respond immediately to these distractions in order to keep us safe.

While threat to safety is no longer a key concern for the modern-day individual, it is how our brains continue to function by default, and it is our responsibility to train our minds to concentrate better.

We all want to function at our highest levels of productivity and realize the most of our potential. What gets in our way of doing so? Why aren't we able to focus?

Here are some common reasons which might be affecting your ability to focus:

1. You don't know how to prioritize, or aim to do too much at once
2. You're switching from once task to another
3. You're doing more than one thing at one time, with limited attention towards each
4. You're not motivated or have lost passion for the task at hand
5. You're constantly distracted, by social media, by your environment, or by any other external triggers
6. You've stretched yourself too much and are overworked or burnt-out
7. You aren't well-rested, or have a poor diet, or have an unhealthy lifestyle that is hampering your ability to concentrate

Understanding what makes you lose your focus can give you a much better chance of setting yourself up for success.

Quick check

What's making you lose your focus? List the top three reasons:

A: 1. _____

    2. _____

    3. _____

What's the best way to figure out what to focus on?

It's entirely possible that you understand the importance of focus, but as millions of other people around the world, you're inundated with choices, and your real problem is that *you don't know what to focus on*. You don't know which of your many choices or potential paths you want to commit to. It's not a lack of enthusiasm, but rather a lack of direction that keeps you from concentrating on the single most important thing.

So, how do you decide what to focus on, and what to let go (at least for the time being?)

You choose what to focus on by choosing the right goals, for the right reasons.

You want to think about all your goals, articulate them as best as you can, and think about why you want to achieve them.

If you don't know what your target is, you won't be able to hit it! And if you don't know *why* you're chasing after something, or if you're chasing it for the wrong reasons, you're likely to give up your pursuit sooner rather than later.

For instance, let's say you want to read more. You probably want to read more because you want to learn more. So rather than setting your goal as 'I want to read 100 books this year', it might be a better idea to set your goal as 'I want to absorb and learn as much as I can from the books I read.'

Setting clear goals, for the right reasons, can help you break them down even further, giving you a definite roadmap of what you want to focus on, as well as helping you stay motivated to stay focused.

Further, articulating your goals and why they're important to you, helps you prioritize better amongst many goals you may have in mind, thus improving your chances of being able to tackle them one by one, each time with complete focus.

Spend some time thinking about the top three goals you have in mind. What are these goals, and why do you want to achieve each one?

A: 1. _____ , _____

   2. _____ , _____

   3. _____ , _____

Based on your above thoughts, pick one goal you want to focus on for the next thirty days, and break it down:

A: Your goal _____

Your reason for pursuing the goal _____

What are the immediate next steps you need to focus on to achieve the goal?

1.

2.

3.

4.

Why Focus Matters

"Whenever you want to achieve something, keep your eyes open, concentrate and make sure you know exactly what it is you want. No one can hit their target with their eyes closed."

Paulo Coelho

We live in an increasingly chaotic world, with multiple distractions screaming for our attention every minute. We live carrying unprecedented levels of stress, amidst ubiquitous advertisements broadcasted by thousands of brands and social media updates. On top of that, with connectivity for work made possible across borders and time zones with the Internet - it's never been harder to focus. And it's never been more necessary, either!

Distraction has become an addictive way of life. The mind is constantly challenged to stay fixed on the task at hand. The quicker and more frequently we lose our focus—according to studies about every eight minutes—we need to regain it back. Different studies cite different time spans needed for an individual to regain focus once it's been broken. Some say it takes just 5 minutes, while others say it takes up to 25 minutes.

Multiply this with the number of times an individual is typically distracted in a day, and you can see how much time is lost in just getting back to the task, owing to distractions and feeding the mind with instant gratification. Now multiply this over a person's life span, and you'll see how this lost time compounds!

Why does focus matter in the long-term?

You may have heard the saying, *'you become what you focus on'*. What catches and consumes your attention creates your thoughts. Your thoughts impact your emotions and desires, and these in turn drive your decisions, behavior and your actions, which influence the series of outcomes that make up your life.

In other words, the way your life unfolds in the long-term begins with what you focus on. Most of us take our day-to-day choices, and how we use our time and our minds, for granted. We don't understand that these become habitual patterns and we don't comprehend the significance these will have on our lives in the long run.

For instance, let's say it's a Saturday. Do you want to watch an episode on Netflix, or an informative TED talk presentation? This doesn't seem like the choice matters a lot. Let's say you go ahead with the episode. Now, let's say you make the same choice on Sunday as well. And let's say you do that every weekend this month, and next month, and for the rest of the year. In the end, you'll end up watching 100+ episodes of some show you can't remember, when you could have watched 104 TED talks instead. Think about how much you would have learnt!

The philosopher Epictetus, in his work 'The Art of Living', once said *"If you yourself don't choose what thoughts and images you expose yourself to, someone else will, and their motives may not be the highest"*.

It is entirely in your control, and completely your responsibility, to choose what you focus on and what you feed your mind with. Once you've grasped that the way your life unfolds begins with—and depends on—your thoughts, you won't overlook the significance of paying attention to the right things.

The best part of this is that even though it might seem impossibly difficult to do at times, each one of us has the power to *choose our thoughts*. Our brains are dynamic and malleable; our thoughts, feelings and experiences are continuously shaping them and re-shaping them.

Experiences and repetitive thoughts activate neural connections. The thoughts we focus on repeatedly ensure that some neural connections are fired up again and again. Over time, some of these strengthen; that's why you recall some memories a lot more vividly than others.

We have to strive to control our thoughts, and not let our thoughts control us; we have to maximize the power of our 'mind potential' with consistent and conscious effort.

Being human is a deeply complex, unimaginably beautiful, and an endlessly fascinating experience, and much more of this experience is born from within our own minds than we consciously notice. I encourage you to practice the habit of becoming self-aware of what exactly you are focusing on in the moment.

Harnessing the power of focus and of consciously creating our thoughts, can help us unleash the very best versions of ourselves, helping us turn our wildest dreams into a vivid reality. It all starts with what you choose to focus on!

How does focus help in the short-term?

Here's a quick recap of the immediate benefits of focusing on your tasks:

1. It encourages you to prioritize

2. It helps you to complete tasks one by one, as opposed to switching from one incomplete task to another (aka multi-tasking).

3. It helps you save valuable time

4. It helps you reduce errors and improve the quality of your work

5. It improves your chances of success at any given task

6. It helps to reduce your levels of anxiety, stress and frustration

7. It is integral to your mental wellbeing, discipline, and self-care

The Different Types of Focus

"A leader tuned out of his internal world will be rudderless; one blind to the world of others will be clueless; those indifferent to the larger systems within which they operate will be blindsided."

—**Daniel Goleman**, bestselling author of
Focus, The Hidden Driver of Excellence

Your brain is being bombarded with information and stimuli non-stop. It's constantly filtering out what it deems irrelevant, and constantly choosing what to focus on and what to process.

Here are 7 different forms in which your mind tries to focus:

1. Internal Focus

Internal focus refers to a sense of direction, composure, and concentration that comes from within an individual. You might come across people who seem centered, 'in control' or 'on top of things' – these are the people who are operating from a high level of internal focus. They have a clear set of guiding values and principles, and often a strong sense of intuition.

In his book *The Organized Mind*, psychologist Daniel Levitin refers to an 'internal locus of control'. An individual who believes that her locus or center of control lies within her believes that she is entirely in charge of her life and is responsible for the way in which it unfolds.

People with a high degree of internal focus hold themselves accountable for their thoughts, actions and outcomes, and tend not to blame external triggers, circumstances or fate.

With continuous practice, you are capable of building a strong sense of internal focus by training your mind. It's not necessarily easy to do; it requires questioning deeply held beliefs and patterns of conditioning you've had for decades. It requires re-wiring your mind so that every thought resonates with accountability. This is why you must work on your mind harder than anything else. You must train your mind to obey your commands and direction, instead of being led by random thoughts leading you down endless rabbit trails.

Many people, as they go along life, begin to see themselves as victims. In many cases, this might even be true, but a victim-based approach to life sabotages your opportunity to live with focus, clarity and purpose.

You want to constantly try to encourage—within your mind—an internal dialogue that is so powerful and well channeled that external triggers or stimuli don't throw you off course or cause you to have a breakdown.

Strategy #1: Sharpen your internal focus (and separate the relevant from the irrelevant)

Practice meditation. A daily practice of meditation will help you become more aware of your thoughts. Learn how to improve your control over your thoughts with the help of regulating your breathing.

Focusing on a sensory experience such as breathing helps to ensure that you don't let your mind wander. With practice, you develop greater control over your thoughts, and improve the quality of thinking that runs through your mind.

2. External Focus

The human brain has learnt, over millions of years, how to navigate the larger world. Besides honing upon the focus and direction that comes from within, you need to focus on your outer world to live a full life, to make the most of the opportunities that come your way, and in some cases, to simply survive.

You want to refine how aware you are of the world outside you. Are you able to pay complete attention to what your colleagues are saying? Are you entirely immersed in that football game? At that Sunday evening party, are you enjoying yourself thoroughly without thinking about the meeting the next day? If you are, you have an excellent sense of external focus.

Many people aren't entirely present to what's happening around them, even if it is a one-on-one conversation; they're caught up within the chatter of their own minds. External focus is just as crucial as an element of success and progress as internal focus is.

Strategy #2: Hone your external focus – stop living inside your head

Gradually build awareness of what's around you. A great way to start is by paying attention to—and subsequently breaking—the bad habits or patterns you have going on autopilot. Sometimes the best way to start building awareness of the world around you is to shake up the way you've become accustomed to doing things; the way you're doing them may not be optimum or efficient, and in some cases, what you're doing may not even be necessary.

Break out of your rut. Change your wardrobe. Listen to different music. Talk to a stranger. Take a class on a subject that makes you uncomfortable. As you get out of the comfort zone you've grown to live in, you'll be able to notice your mind slowly expanding.

3. Peripheral Focus

An individual with a strong sense of peripheral focus is able to perceive and process many things in his surroundings simultaneously. There are instances where you might need to focus on one thing at a time (for instance, when you're writing an exam paper), and others where you need to focus on multiple things at a time (such as while playing at a basketball tournament). Sportspeople and martial artists have excellent peripheral focus; their victory depends on having honed this ability better than their opponents have.

Strategy #3: Learn how to observe and process many things simultaneously

You can try to improve your peripheral focus in many ways; a great way to start is by practicing peripheral vision. Try to see more, to observe more. Try to do a quick exercise outdoors, perhaps on a park bench.

Sit at a quiet spot, and with a deep breath, try to still your mind. Now try to pay attention not to directly what's ahead of you, but what's surrounding it. Look around; what's to the right? what's above?

You'll instinctively want to focus on the object directly in front, but you want to keep trying to focus on its periphery. Keep repeating this exercise for a couple of minutes each day, and your ability to see and absorb more and more will gradually improve.

4. Narrow Focus

Narrow focus refers to a laser-like focus on one thing at the expense of all else. It is the repetitive and channeled thought and energy directed towards one thing only. Think about a martial artist trying to break a stack of bricks with one swift motion.

Narrow focus comes from rehearsal, from the continuous and challenging practice of a technique. It comes from staying on course to achieve one specific outcome, no matter how long it takes, with the necessary effort and discipline devoted to its accomplishment.

Strategy #4: Learn how to develop laser-like focus through practice

Focusing on one particular thing, and gradually building momentum to gain excellence at achieving it, can deliver outstanding results. Don't be afraid to start small. Create a goal – it could be anything you want to learn or improve at or even stop doing, and break this goal down into smaller parts, with a specific deadline for each.

Slot out time every day—it could be just a couple of minutes to begin with—and dedicate time to your goal. In the following week, increase the time you've allotted. In the following month, increase it even more, and continue expanding. Before you know it, you'll find yourself immersed in the activity more and more, with a rising level of sharp focus.

5. Voluntary Focus

When you consciously set a goal for yourself, with the big picture in mind and total commitment, you're operating out of voluntary focus. You want all your focus to be voluntary, in the sense that you want to control what you focus on, instead of it going the other way around.

When you're developing a 5-year plan for your company, setting out the itinerary for your trip, or deciding on your outfit for the day, you're exhibiting voluntary focus.

Strategy #5: Improve your hold over voluntary focus and learn to cut out the noise

Pick a simple goal – perhaps an item on your daily to-do list—that can be done in ten minutes or less. Write it down and pin it up, or jot it on a sticky note and tack it to your laptop.

Now, focus on this goal and only this goal for the next 5-10 minutes. Let any other thoughts come and go freely; don't resist them as they will only nudge you more if you do. Try to keep bringing your focus back to the goal at hand – by doing so repeatedly, you'll refine your voluntary focus and train your brain to stay on point.

6. Stimulus-based Focus

You may find that your mind isn't able to concentrate on the task at hand but actually jumps to each stimulus as it happens in real time. Maybe it's that email notification on your watch, or the notification update on your phone. Did Elon Musk just tweet something new?

If you can relate to this constant form getting pulled into miscellaneous stimuli and feeling compelled to respond to each one, you're working out of stimulus-based focus. It's also known as 'bottom up' focus because it takes your mind away from its top-down, goal-driven approach and lures it into distraction.

Strategy #6: Learn to control your response to stimuli

A simple technique to resist the temptation from distractions is the *counting technique*. In response to any trigger, such as a WhatsApp ping or a negative thought, pause and count to five. Resist the immediate reaction you've been trained to respond to and break that chain in your mind.

After 5 counts, you'll find it easier to return to the task you had at hand. Even better – adopt this simple yoga practice: count silently forward as you breathe in (1, 2, 3...), and then backward as you breathe out (... 3, 2, 1), and repeat this until you feel calmer.

The more you can control and delay your reaction, the better you're becoming at winning over and reversing the distraction habit.

7. Emotional Focus

Human beings are social creatures – all of us have an inherent need to be understood and to be liked. Also known as 'other' focus or 'relationship' focus, emotion focus refers to your ability to shift attention from within your own self to the person in front of you, thus allowing you to better relate to and connect with them. You may know of some people who come across as deeply empathetic.

They just seem to get you. They appear kind and compassionate, and you love being around them. You can *feel* their energy. These people have excellent emotion focus – they connect very well with others, because they're able to view things from perspectives different from their own.

Strategy #7: Increase your level of empathy and learn to focus on others

Think of the most empathetic person you know (whether real or fictional). Articulate the qualities this person has that you admire the most. Is it a soothing voice? Is it their expressiveness? Is it their easy-going demeanor? What do you think makes this person different?

As the next step, think about the qualities that you most admire in general. As you interact with people, try to spot and to focus on the good qualities they have that you admire, as opposed to the bad. Over time, you'll improve your emotion focus. Not only will your quality of interactions improve, but you'll also feel much better within!

Your mind can be a source that drives unparalleled accomplishment, or it can be a prison for your motivation. Your thoughts can elevate you by building and revealing the best you can be, or they can spiral away without any brakes, and break you down completely.

Growth always makes rapid progress with the positive thoughts you choose to focus on.

You must aim to carefully develop balance between your internal and external focus, as well as your peripheral and narrow focus. You don't want to be lost in your internal world when you need to focus on important tasks at hand. And neither do you want to be at the mercy of external triggers with no control over your own thoughts.

There are times when you'll need to laser in on one thing only; there are other times when you'll need to watch many moving parts at once.

Your brain is capable of miracles - you need to help it by training it in the art of the different types of focus. By developing tough mental discipline, you'll be able to shift focus internally or externally, as and when you need to. And you'll find yourself becoming nothing short of unstoppable in whatever you choose to achieve.

The Process of Building Focus

"Concentrate all your thoughts upon the work at hand. The sun's rays do not burn until brought to a focus."

Alexander Graham Bell

You've understood what focus truly is, why it matters, and how to channel the different forms of focus to your advantage. But how do you go about building focus? Where do you begin? What process do you follow, and how do you ensure your pursuit of building focus is not only fruitful but, is also sustainable and enjoyable?

The key is to begin with one thing to focus on, to complete this task or meet this goal, and then move on to your next pursuit, thus creating a continuous flow of victories, each one fueling the next. Success begets success, and the more wins you rack up, the greater confidence you will develop in your deep focus sessions.

Focus on One Thing Until Done

We've found ourselves in a world where multi-tasking is the norm and focusing on one thing at a time is an exception. However, in doing so, we sacrifice the potential for our brains to level up and cultivate the right mind with the best training.

Conditioning the mind to focus on and accomplish task after task, goal after goal, with the help of the right habits, delivers the outcome you truly desire. Instead of ending up with whatever cheap pleasure that's derived from instant gratification, you reap the benefits of a focused mind trained to execute on priority tasks.

The more we repeatedly do something, the easier it becomes to do; it becomes a pattern, a *good habit*. The scientific term for this practice is 'automaticity'. It's the ability of your mind to let you do something on autopilot. It takes a great deal of effort and time to set up a new habit.

While some studies claim it takes 21 days, others state it takes 66 days and some even say it takes 254 days for a new habit to be fully ingrained in you - but once you've managed to establish a new habit, your activity will be almost automatic. When you focus on one thing only, and one thing after another at a time, each one becomes easier to do as it becomes habitual.

Here are a few techniques which will set you on the path to building focus and sharpening your mind.

Technique 1: Create goals for yourself

It is said that the difference between a dream and a goal is that a dream is a gift you *wish to receive*, whereas a goal is an outcome you *work to achieve*. Without a concrete goal, you can't have a clear plan. Without a plan, your actions will have no particular direction, and your energies will be expended wastefully.

Here are 11 steps to help you identify, articulate, and clearly define your goals:

1. Begin with an idea dump. List out all the things you've wanted to achieve, without setting any limitations in your mind.

2. Choose your master goal. What is it that you want the most in your life? Don't winnow it down – be bold in what you're asking of yourself, and trust that you will figure out a way to make it happen. Once you've chosen your master goal, write it down and commit to it.

3. Put a timeline to your goal. It doesn't matter if it is 2 months, 2 years, or 20 years – but put a definite timeline.

4. Break down your big goal. What will you need to accomplish in the next 1 year? Reverse engineer your big goal by writing down all the steps necessary to achieve it (hence, the next step).

5. Break your big goal down into 'sub-goals'. Make a list of every task, no matter how small, and identify what it is and how much time required to finish it. Think of this as your to-do list – what

simple tasks will help you move towards accomplishing your goal?

6. Prioritize your action steps. What do you need to do right away, and what's not as urgent?

7. Visualize your success daily. Feeling how you would feel once you've accomplished your goal will fuel you to work towards it.

8. Become part of a supportive community. Invite accountability into your lifestyle. You don't have to do everything all by yourself!

9. Be mindful of your obstacles. Are you missing key resources? Do you hold limiting beliefs that are sabotaging you in your quest? Be honest and list out your obstacles so that you can find ways to overcome them.

10. Identify the skills and knowledge you need to reach your goal.

11. Continuously and honestly review your progress. Set up weekly and monthly review sessions to get an accurate benchmark of your progress.

Follow these steps and you should be well on your way to building an extraordinary level of focus.

Technique 2: Build 'focus blocks' to improve productivity

Using 'focus blocks' refers to chalking out chunks of time on your calendar for specific activities. Doing your taxes? Block out time on your calendar. Brainstorming ideas for your next project? Set aside time. Whatever task is pressing, whether it be attending your child's concert or much-required me-time, you want to dedicate time exclusively to that activity for that particular period of time.

Scheduling time is the easy part – the harder part is to ensure that you work only on that specific activity for that chunk of time, ignoring all else. This includes not checking up on interrupting emails and not pausing for a colleague dropping by for some quick help.

Here are **7 quick tips** to help you:

1. Commit to your scheduling system.

2. Use your calendar, use your stickies, use a daily planner - use every tool at your disposal to help you stick to your system.

3. Make a reasonable schedule – you don't want to burn out in the process of reaching for your optimum level of focus.

4. Get your colleagues onboard – you can share your calendar so that they can see when you're available.

5. Find a quiet and comfortable spot to work without distraction.

6. Work in sync with your natural cycle. When do you concentrate best? Set your schedule accordingly.

7. Don't give up. If you find yourself off course, gently bring yourself back to plan.

It's hard to get into the system of working with focus blocks. But, once you commit to it—and discuss it with your colleagues—you can request that they not interrupt, and you'll find a tremendous boost in productivity.

Technique 3: Use focus-building activities in a group setting

While the first two techniques were inward-focused, here's another technique to help you start building better focus, and this one can be group-based. Pick a focus-building activity, and schedule time with friends or family centered around this activity. Think 'puzzle-night'!

You probably worked on a lot of puzzles as a child –puzzles are a great way to stimulate the mind and build focus not only in children, but also in adults.

Here are **five benefits** of using puzzles as a work-out for your brain:

1. Improve cognitive function and spatial reasoning

2. Develop better attention to detail

3. Improve your memory, especially short-term memory

4. Enhance your problem-solving ability and IQ over time

5. Immerse yourself in an esteem-boosting activity and reduce stress

If jigsaw puzzles aren't your thing, you can go with crossword games, solve brain teasers, work with Sudoku, or even use apps such as Luminosity. If you're a chess player, it can be a fantastic way improve focus as well.

No matter which technique you choose to begin your journey of improving your ability to focus, you want to ensure you commit to one thing at a time and stay on course. The process of building focus is an ongoing challenge, but it comes with life-changing rewards that make it totally worth the commitment.

Part II: Eliminate the Obstacles to Focus

"Only through focus can you do world-class things, no matter how capable you are."

Bill Gates

"I don't care how much power, brilliance or energy you have, if you don't harness it and focus it on a specific target and hold it there you're never going to accomplish as much as your ability warrants."

— Zig Ziglar

7 Common Obstacles that Block Focus

*"Focus does not mean saying yes,
it means saying no."*

Steve Jobs

In a world of tweets, reels, posts, emails, hashtags, live stories, and news flashes for everything ranging from the crucial to the absurd, we've come to believe that we have no option but to multitask. It's much harder to ignore things than to quickly respond to them, or at least just check on them! What if that email needs an urgent response?

What if you're the last one to find out your friend's having a baby? Alright – you won't respond if it's not urgent, but why not just take a quick look? You've been doing this day after day, and it's become a way of life.

Here are some statistics that are likely to make you sit up and take notice of just how much you are losing out on because of these continuous distractions.

1. We have, on average, 12,000 – 50,000 thoughts daily. 80% of these thoughts are negative thoughts, made up of concerns such as regrets of the past, worries of the future, comparisons with others, or other forms of complaints.

2. On average, people check their email 15 times a day.

3. On average, people check their phones 96 times a day (or every 10 minutes). For millennials, this number is 150.

4. Around the world, an individual on average spends 2 hours and 24 minutes per day on social media. Calculated over a lifetime, this works out to 6 years and 8 months of their lives spent on social media.

5. The most common cause of road accidents is distracted driving, resulting from activities such as cell-phone usage or eating behind the wheel. Distracted driving causes more crashes every year than speeding or drunk driving.

If you're scared, you're not alone. Our immediate environments, physical and digital, are no longer inherently designed to allow us to focus. You're likely to have heard that you're a product of your environment. Who you've been, who you are, and who you will be is often more closely intertwined with your surroundings than you realize.

The people you spend your time with, the places you spend your time in, the apps you spend your time on, the conditioning you imbibe, the attitudes you develop and the experiences you have – all directly and profoundly impact the level of focus you're able to achieve.

In developing deep focus then, its only right that you begin by *removing* the obstacles that come in the way of allowing you to focus. There are many factors that might be throwing you off course. These could be external, such as a distracting environment, or internal, such as a fear of failure.

Here are the **top 7 ways in which** focus is commonly disrupted. Take a look - which ones ring a bell? Get rid of all your obstacles one by one; as the noise dies down, you'll find an immediate boost in your ability to get things done.

Obstacle 1: A conflicting environment that doesn't support a productive workflow

Your trainer has asked you to complete 30 reps by the time he's back. But before you get started – why not take a quick look at Instagram for those pictures from the dinner last night? It's the middle of the day and you should have been halfway through that report. But your colleague is raving about that new show on Netflix – maybe you should just take a peek at the trailer... Sound familiar?

Maybe you sit so close to the coffee machine that you can't *not* overhear all that gossip. It's possible that the TV screen is placed at an angle that always distracts you. Perhaps you're allergic to that new car fragrance. Maybe your work desk is so cluttered you can't ever find what you need.

There could be a variety of stimulants distracting you day after day, keeping you from your goals, breaking your chain of thought, or reducing your efficiency, in some cases without your even realizing it.

When your environment is intentionally designed with the goal of reducing irrelevant stimuli and helping you concentrate, no matter the task at hand, you'll accomplish everything much more seamlessly.

Don't underestimate the need to design the right environment – it matters, *a lot*. No one can be 100% motivated every single day, and we live in an age that is more interconnected and more informative than ever before. Getting the *outside* right *will* help make things easier *inside* your mind.

Identifying your distractors: Refining your environment for better focus

Think about the **physical environments** you spend a lot of time in. Your desk, your kitchen, your car – what keeps distracting you in these spaces?

What would you change in these spaces? How can you clear out the clutter?

It's equally important to evaluate your **digital environment**. Your phone will probably show you how much time you spend on each app last week. Are you happy with what you find?

What apps do you need to spend less time on?

The **people** you constantly interact with (physically or virtually) can elevate you or bring you down. Who are the 5 people you spend most of your time with?

Which people bring out the best in you and how can you spend more time with them?

Obstacle 2: Lack of clarity around your #1 goal and priority for that day

How often do you jump out of bed each day, clearly knowing the ONE big thing you want to accomplish? It could be as tricky as having that appraisal conversation with your boss. Or as delightful as a bubble bath with your baby. Or as challenging as your first headstand after a year of yoga.

No matter what it may be, if you don't have a clear goal for most of your days, no matter the area of your life it falls under, like most people, you aren't seizing the day!

Many people simply go through life day after day, with each day being the same as the previous one, and before they know it, each year has been the same as the previous year. If you're like 95% of our society, you will settle for less than what you want out of your life and will go through life without realizing your true potential.

If you want to be a part of the remaining 5%, you need to live each day with a sense of purpose and motivation, and you need clarity of thought with regards to your goals. Take life one day at a time, but try to make the most of each day, and you'll find yourself living a better life than most people around you.

Quick check

- What was your #1 priority yesterday? A: _____
- Did you meet your goal? A: _____
- What went right/wrong? A: _____
- What will you prioritize for tomorrow? A: _____

Obstacle 3: Too many ideas pulling at your attention

Have you had days where you have so much to do that you don't know where to get started? You know you can't afford to waste a single minute, and yet by the end of the day you haven't managed to get *any* of it done?

When you're all geared up it might seem like a great idea to make an ambitious to-do list, or work on multiple new ideas at once. One of the biggest obstacles to focus, however, is making the mistake of not knowing what to prioritise and, losing your concentration in trying to do too much all at once. 98% of the people around the world are *not* effective multitaskers. The odds are clearly not on your side!

Eliminating what's not urgent and working on one idea or goal at a time helps you keep your eyes on the prize. Whether your new intern messes up, or you come up with a mind-blowing new idea in the shower, or you find you've received 50 emails over the weekend won't matter – your mind will find a way to bring you back to the all-important task at hand for the day, and you'll make time on your calendar for your other ideas.

Do this day after day, and at the end of the month – voila! You'll find you really did meet all of those items on your agenda after all, because you worked on one idea at a time and did justice to each one.

Here's an easy exercise that will help you articulate your top ideas and improve your chances of executing each one.

- What are the top 10 ideas/goals on your mind right now?
- Rewrite these in the order of importance to you.
- Put an end date for each – mark it out on your calendar, whether it's a day from now, or a year away.

Obstacle 4: An unhealthy attitude towards failure

Most of us erroneously believe, whether consciously or subconsciously, that the way things have been in the past is the way things will be in the future. **If something hasn't happened in the past, we assume it won't in the future.** Or conversely, we expect that **something that has already happened will happen again**. If you've succeeded at something in the past, you'll feel more confident about it, but if you failed at it, you'll be hesitant to re-attempt it.

It is human to fail. If you aren't failing, it means you are not trying your hand at something new, or aren't aiming high enough. Any successful person will tell you that failure is the precursor to success. It isn't something to worry about or try to dodge – it is, in many ways, inevitable and necessary.

An individual who has never failed, has never had the chance to build resilience. Conversely, if you've failed at something that was important to you and have overcome it, chances are you've learnt invaluable lessons and shown a great deal of courage in re-attempting your pursuit.

We could fail across any aspect of our lives, be it at school, in our relationships, with our money, in our business, at our job, with our friends, or with any other important people in our lives. The most resilient and successful people in the world – no matter what area of life you're looking at – will tell you that failure it nothing but re-direction.

Failing teaches you what *not* to do, and what to focus on instead. It's an opportunity to try again, this time, from a place of more wisdom.

Adopting a positive attitude towards failure and eliminating the fear of failure from your mind can help you overcome a common obstacle to focus. In a work setting, this can help not only you, but also your team.

Quick check

Here's a quick survey that will help you articulate your own attitude towards failure, as well as capture that of your team:

- What do you think it means to fail? What do you think should happen after you fail?
- What adjustment would you like to make in your own thinking, and in the overall values / attitudes of your team towards failure and success? Remember that taking away the fear of failure can help you and your team operate at a whole new level of focus.
- Ask five of your closest friends what they think it means to fail? Now, ask five people in your company or organization? People

have different perspectives on failure. Some embrace the experience, and many more run from it or avoid it completely by doing what is easy.

Obstacle 5: Not sticking with consistency of the work habit

You may have discovered that you've started out with something with a lot of enthusiasm, only to abandon the task, or to leave it unresolved, hoping to come back to it later, only that you never do. Or you may have found that you jump from one idea to another one that seems more interesting.

For some tasks, such as starting a new work-out, you may find that the hardest part is to begin. For others, such as completing a project report, the hard part might be sticking with it until it's finished.

It's important to complete tasks, both for your own mental set-up, and for how others perceive you. Here's why it's important to stay consistent and to ensure that you complete your tasks:

- You build a sense of control and confidence when you complete what you begin

- You don't waste your time in revisiting the activity, figuring out which bits you had finished and remembering what you need to do next

- You build a sense of fulfilment

- You learn how to take up more responsibility

- You reduce for yourself the anxiety that builds up from continuous procrastination

- You earn the confidence of those who entrusted you with the task

- You keep your word to yourself and to others

When you're continuously working with consistency, taking up one challenge after another and ticking off one to-do item after another, you'll find your confidence soar and your focus enhanced.

Break the habit of leaving things mid-way, and build consistency in all you do, whether it's a simple chore or a big project. Here's an easy exercise to help you identify what you're leaving unfinished (and why).

- What were the last five things you set out to do?
- Mark out which ones you completed right away and which ones you postponed.
- For the completed tasks – note what you enjoyed about them, so that you can take up more.
- For the incomplete tasks – articulate why you **procrastinated**.
- How do you plan to resolve the incomplete tasks, and how will you deal with similar tasks in the future?

For instance, you could re-schedule tasks that are not pressing for the weekend. Some other tasks, you could delegate or outsource.

Obstacle 6: A lifestyle that causes stress and mental exhaustion

*"Lack of direction, not lack of time, is the problem.
We all have twenty-four hour days."*

Zig Ziglar

Stress and anxiety take away valuable mental energy and are massive barriers to focus. If you're mentally and emotionally exhausted, you're naturally going to expend a lot more effort to get the same task completed. Its deeply worrying that almost 20% of the population of the United States suffers from some form of anxiety disorder.

We're continuously worried about something or the other, whether it's about our work, about our relationships, about our health, about our finances, about what others are doing, or about what someone thinks of us. It's exhausting and a continuous obstruction of valuable mental real estate.

People who succeed more often or who are more content in life don't have more time on their hands. In many cases, they have no inherent or gifted undue advantage either. But all of them have *cultivated* an edge for themselves by doing what most others won't – they've developed an ability for laser-like focus. They've found clarity with regard to exactly what they want, committed to it in entirety, and left themselves with no option other than to succeed.

When you're able to overcome the obstacle of anxiety and are able to free up your mind, you'll give yourself the chance to build a similar competitive advantage as well.

Here is a list of common anxiety-inducing triggers for people around the world that drain their mental energy. Which ones do you relate to, and what specific actions can you take to alleviate your worries?

Triggers that may be inducing anxiety within you:

- Health / medication issues
- Caffeine / lack of sleep
- Financial matters
- Social events
- Arguments and conflicts with a partner, relative, friend or colleague
- Work-related issues or relationships
- School-related issues or relationships
- A discomfort with uncertainty
- A traumatic past experience
- An addiction to Drugs, alcohol, pornography, etc....

If you do feel anxiety due to any trigger, what can you do to reduce it? For instance, you could ask your doctor for different medication. Or you could limit the amount of caffeine you take in. Financial discomfort? Map out a savings or investment plan.

The bottom line is, you must take intentional action towards the results you intend to achieve.

Obstacle 7: Allowing physical exhaustion

Besides mental exhaustion, a major impediment to your focus could be a lack of physical energy. A study reports that only one in seven Americans say that they feel fresh when they wake up every day of the week. We're doing way too much all the time, and we'll yet have a ton more left to do.

A healthy body contributes to a healthy mind. Conversely, if you're feeling physically drained, you're unlikely to be able to concentrate. You might be feeling ill, drowsy, or simply apathetic. You might be sleep deprived, vitamin deficient, or overworked, all of which will take a toll on your body and in turn, your mind.

The mind and body are intertwined; your brain generates the thoughts and emotions which affect your body. Conversely, physical practices such as pranayama meditation have proved to show not only physiological, but also neurological changes.

Different signals originating in your physical body are detected by your nervous system, and in turn can modulate your feelings. It is you and only you that can control all the dimensions of your being – your body, your mind, and your emotions.

As stated in the ancient Hindu text, the Gita, *"the self is the friend of the self. The self has to be raised by the self."*

Quick check

Similar to the previous exercise on alleviating anxiety, here's a quick to-do for you to identify and address your key causes of physical exhaustion.

Triggers that may be causing you to constantly feel physically tired:

- An unhealthy diet (for instance, an intake of too many refined carbs)

- Not enough physical movement (sitting or lying down too much)
- Fatigue due to food sensitivity to specific items
- Mental fatigue due to chronic stress
- Lack of sleep (this is probably the #1 reason for many people)
- Not enough protein / not enough food / not enough hydration
- Vitamin deficiency
- Being overweight and/or overeating
- Diabetes, glandular fever, or another health condition
- Inadequate exercise

What can you do to address this cause? What changes do you need to make?

Part III:

The Focus Mindset

"Take up one idea. Make that one idea your life — think of it; dream of it; live on that idea. Let the brain, muscles, nerves, every part of your body, be full of that idea; and leave every other idea alone. This is the way to success."

Swami Vivekananda

"A major stimulant to creative thinking is focused questions. There is something about a well-worded question that often penetrates to the heart of the matter and triggers new ideas and insights."

— **Brian Tracy,** bestselling author of *Eat That Frog!*

Controlling the Fear of Failure

"When you take risks, you learn that there will be times when you succeed and there will be times when you fail, and both are equally important."

Ellen DeGeneres

You've heard this time and again – *it all starts in your mind*. The way you talk to yourself and the thoughts you allow and empower creates your mindset. Anything approached with a mindset which is healthy and positive can make the task at hand easier to accomplish; a negative mindset can slow down, derail or even sabotage whatever you set out to do.

Before you can learn and master specific strategies that will help you to build deep focus, prepping yourself by getting into the right mindset can prove to be extremely helpful. You want to unleash your highest level of focus, and *remain* that focused, *on purpose*. What is the right frame of mind that can make it easier for you to do so?

Mindset and the Fear of Failure

A major mindset shift that most people require to make as they begin their journey towards building focus is to get rid of their fear of failure. Fear is one of the most powerful of all human instincts, instilled in us as part of our evolution to help us survive.

When used as a tool, fear is useful; it nudges us to protect ourselves and helps us spot threats to our wellbeing. However, for most of us, fear ends up becoming an obstacle, keeping us from our fullest potential and from chasing our dreams.

Failure is different things to different people, simply because each of us is a blend of a completely distinct set of ideas, hopes, strengths, weaknesses, values and conditioning patterns. A failure in one context could be a smashing success in a different setting, and what one person thinks of as a failure could be a huge win for another.

What makes you afraid to fail? Where does your fear of failure come from? In many cases, people may not even know that they're operating from a fear of failure. For instance, do any of the below sound familiar?

- You constantly think about what others will think about you – this could be your parents, your friends, your colleagues, or your children

- You're often sabotaging your own efforts by procrastinating or worrying excessively

- You feel like you're not good enough

- Others have often told you that you have low self-esteem or self-confidence

- You don't like to attempt new things and stay away from challenges

- You're a perfectionist and will only try your hand at things you're sure to succeed at

- You're highly influenced by a perfectionist, and this affects what tasks you take on

- You believe you have a reputation to maintain and are afraid to do anything that will affect it

- You've had a traumatic past experience that influences all your present choices

All of these are symptoms of the **fear of failure**. Any of these could be hampering your thoughts and actions, whether consciously or subconsciously.

Be truly honest with yourself and spend some time trying to identify exactly what it is that makes you afraid. Some of the answers might make you uncomfortable, but by doing this you're taking the first step in committing to your growth and to building a focus mindset.

Overcoming Fear and Embracing Failure

Once you've analyzed where your fear of failure comes from, it's time to fight it and get rid of it! It will take effort, time, and consistency on your part but once you've released your fears, you'll begin to make massive leaps in your growth.

Here are five ways to help you control your fear:

1. **Build clarity** – What exactly do you wish to accomplish, and why? When you're clear in your own goals, and committed and impassioned with chasing them, you're less likely to look left and right, less likely to look behind, and more interested in moving forward.
2. **Think of the worst-case scenario** – What's the absolute worst thing that could happen? Chances are, it's not all that bad! The philosopher Seneca once said, *"we suffer more in imagination than in reality"*. Your imagination is powerful – don't misuse it.
3. **Imagine multiple scenarios** – A great deal of fear arises because outcomes are unknown, and most of us are not well-equipped to deal with uncertainty. Spend time and enlist as many scenarios as you can imagine – good and bad. This helps you feel less uncertain, and more comfortable with the way things might unfold.
4. **Have a back-up plan** – Having a plan B, as long as it isn't distracting you, might be a great way to cope with being afraid. If you have something wonderful to fall back on, you're less likely to fear failure.
5. **Start small** – Don't worry about what's at the top of the ladder, just try to take the first step, keep going, and trust in yourself and in your choices, one incremental step at a time.

Fight the Scarcity Mindset and Focus on Abundance

Another big factor that may be instilling a fear of failure in you is that you may be focusing on scarcity instead of seeing the abundance around you. You might have come to believe that one's loss is another's gain, and that both can't win.

While this might certainly be true from a very short-term perspective, in the larger scheme of things there is absolutely no limit to the opportunities the world offers, or to the circumstances and the possibilities that might come your way.

A mindset focused on what you're losing or have lost can keep you from being able to spot an opportunity that might be a thousand times better or, might be better in a thousand different ways. Once you train your mind to spot opportunities and abundance instead of limitations and boundaries, you're stepping up to a new level in your journey of growth.

Here's how you can begin to shift gears from a scarcity mindset to an abundance mindset:

- Focus on what you have, not what you don't have.
- Practice gratitude everyday.
- Surround yourself with people who advise you well and cheer you on.
- Get creative and come up with situations wherein everyone wins.
- Shift your attention to the solutions, instead of fixating on the obstacles.

The most optimistic and most successful people in the world see opportunities where others see chaos; what you see is what you'll act on, so you want to train yourself to see the good and not the undesirable.

Consciously Adopting a Positive Mindset

"The mind is like water. When it's turbulent, it's difficult to see; when it's calm, everything becomes clear."

Prasad Mahes

You may have heard of the phrase 'monkey mind.' It is a Buddhist term that refers to a mind that is unsettled, uncontrolled, restless, and clouded. Your mind can be a weapon when you control and harness it correctly, and it can become your worst enemy if you let it control or paralyze you.

In order to shift to a positive mindset from a negative one, you need to first train your brain to stop monkeying about, so that you can build calmness and awareness. Next, you want to retain this sense of composure by keeping your mind from getting distracted all the time.

With your mind prepped in this manner, you're much more likely to develop an attitude of focusing on solutions instead of problems, enabling you to slowly elevate and revamp your mind and your life.

Control the Monkey Mind

To start building control over your mind, you've got to first stop letting it control you! Here are a couple of ways in which your mind might be trying to control you by repeating thoughts that don't serve your best interests and your progress:

You project past experiences into the future. Your mind may be telling you that you can't do something because you've never done it previously (even though it is something you wish to attempt). You need to consciously and courageously address these negative thoughts – nothing ventured is nothing gained!

You can't break old patterns. Maybe you've always done things a certain way. Maybe you've always gone to that friend's house even though the interactions always pull you down. Maybe you've always read that beauty magazine that leaves you feeling inadequate. Closely evaluate what you're continuously exposing yourself to – what's good for you and what isn't?

You're used to responding to certain triggers in specific ways. Got an email? By default, maybe you check in right away. Take a step back – what IF you check all your emails at specific times twice a day? Become more conscious of your triggers and your responses.

You've gotten into the habit of being the victim. Everyone's lives are easy but yours. Everyone gets what they want, even though they aren't better than you.

If you're going down this train of thought, you've made yourself a victim. Unless you break out of it and take ownership of everything that happens to you, you'll remain at the mercy of thoughts that don't encourage you to grow.

An uncontrolled and unchecked train of negative thoughts can spiral away and leave you feeling exhausted, angry, and dissatisfied. Learn how to control the chatter and the unhelpful and harmful thoughts that fill you with fear. Keep trusting yourself.

Eliminate Shiny Object Syndrome (SOS)

Once you're on your way to training your mind for composure, you want to ensure you allow it to stay that way. You may have heard of Shiny object syndrome (SOS); it's a human tendency to be a part of the new thing – the new trend, or the new big idea. You might have heard of another similar trending term, 'FOMO' or 'Fear Of Missing Out'.

The problem with constantly chasing each new shiny thing is that you lose your composure and your focus. It starts with a distraction, and then you find yourself immersed in it at the expense of what you should have been doing. You end up procrastinating, which results in your stress levels rising, leaving you overwhelmed.

Stop allowing your mind to get distracted by eliminating both SOS and FOMO and retain the focus you've worked so hard to build.

Here are several ways to help you overcome SOS:

- Take complete ownership of your actions and your decisions.
- Be grateful for the things you do have, that many others might never have.
- Don't compare yourself with others.
- Learn to say 'no' without fear of the consequences.
- Get rid of the constant distractions and triggers completely and set aside time to get around to these in a manner that doesn't impede your focus.

Focus on the Solution

As humans, since we've evolved to pay deep attention to threats and problems, we're biased towards negativity more than we are towards positivity; immediately reacting to problems is hardwired in our systems and we do it almost automatically.

For instance, you may realize that you tend to remember insults more than you remember praises. Or that you remember bad memories more vividly than good ones. This phenomenon is also called 'positive – negative asymmetry.' Understanding that our brains were programmed in a certain way through millions of years can help us re-train it better when it's not serving us in line with our best interests.

Here are seven ways in which you can begin to **shift your focus** towards a solution-oriented and optimistic frame of mind, as opposed to dwelling on threats and problems:

1. Turn the situation around and look at it from a different perspective
2. Put an end to hurtful self-talk and harmful beliefs
3. Enjoy the present moment and be grateful for all that is well
4. Set aside time just to ideate and brainstorm; come up with different ways to tackle your problems
5. If something simply hasn't been working, change it and incorporate more of what does work

6. Take one step at a time and let each one build on the previous one
7. Get help. Reach out to positive, uplifting and like-minded people

Break up a long-term problem. What immediate actions can you take to move towards the solution to the problem? For example, your problem may be that you're twenty pounds overweight for a wedding next year. Instead of worrying about it, decide to have a healthy meal tonight.

Let go of negative thoughts that are doing absolutely nothing to serve your present happiness or your future growth. Committing to building and retaining mental equanimity and developing a solution-oriented mindset will transform your life, bringing you energy and enthusiasm the likes of which you may have never previously felt!

Getting into the Focus Zone

"My mind isn't wandering. I am not thinking of something else. I am totally involved in what I am doing. My body feels good. I don't seem to hear anything. The world seems to be cut off from me. I am less aware of myself and my problems. The ego falls away. Time flies. Every action, movement, and thought follows inevitably from the previous one, like playing jazz."

Mihaly Csikszentmihalyi, on the state of being 'in flow'

In psychology, 'flow' refers to a mental state wherein one is completely engrossed and focused for a certain period of time on something specific. Additionally, it is a positive experience, and even a joyful one.

A psychologist called Mihaly Csikszentmihalyi is credited for having brought this concept of flow to the masses. You might have found yourself, at some point in time, in this state of deep flow, or 'in the zone.' Chances are, it felt great! You might have even had a similar feeling after an excellent meditation or yoga session.

In your journey to build a focused mind, it can be tremendously helpful to learn how to get into, or induce, this state of flow for yourself. It's a mental state wherein you'll find yourself clear, aware, balanced, composed, controlled, and concentrating completely on your actions, oblivious to miscellaneous problems, without one eye on the time and half your mind thinking of something else. Naturally, this will leave you feeling happy and fulfilled.

Creating the Deep Flow State

Here are six tips to help you work your way into a state of deep flow:

1. Ensure you love what you're doing. If you simply don't care about what needs to be done, you won't be invested in a successful outcome
2. Give yourself time to prepare. Use meditation, chanting, exercising, or running – whatever helps you get ready to take on something challenging.

3. Don't worry about the result and learn to enjoy the process. If a painter were more focused on how successful her gallery exhibit will be as opposed to the strokes she's making, she isn't bringing her best to the canvas board.
4. Know your 'why'. Knowing what drives you acts as fuel and keeps you from giving up the moment something becomes hard or boring.
5. Ensure an environment in which you aren't interrupted. Close that door. Put that phone on airplane mode. Put up that 'do not disturb' sign. Turn off notifications for those social media apps. Update your calendar for time slots where you don't want to be disturbed.
6. Work in sync with your natural mental cycle, scheduling the most challenging work for times when you're at your productive best and when your mind is most likely to be able to concentrate fully.

Use music for getting into (and staying in) focused flow

An excellent tool to help you get into (and stay in) a state of deep flow is music. As you can imagine, different kinds of music can evoke different emotions, thoughts, and mental states in you.

Additionally, the same kind of music can be helpful in one setting but distracting in another. For example, you might find music with lyrics distracting when you're trying to read something complex, but you might welcome it during an intense work-out. Music can be uplifting or relaxing, distracting or calming, depending on what you choose to hear at what instance.

Certain kinds of music have been found to be extremely helpful in uplifting people's moods and boosting their concentration; you can explore music within these categories to find what works best in inducing you into your focused flow state:

Nature music

Sounds of nature as ambient music can be very soothing. Used extensively for therapies and meditation practices, sounds that evoke waves, rainfall, and gardens are often excellent choices to uplift your mood, calm you down, and help you focus.

Classical music

Einstein, one of the greatest minds to have ever lived, was an ardent fan of Mozart and Bach, and famously spent a great deal of time on his violin, which he had named 'Lina'. Listening to classical music can help boost your brain, and research has confirmed that it positively enhances aptitude for specific activities, such as solving spatial puzzles.

Cinematic music

Another kind of music that can help get you into your deep flow state is instrumental cinematic music. Depending on the soundtrack you choose, it could help you feel adventurous, emboldened, or inspired, putting you in your best mood to execute your task.

Once you've learnt how to get yourself into a state of deep flow, and you do so repeatedly, you'll begin to enjoy your routine and your process, which will naturally bring you the results you desire. This in turn will motivate you to chase bigger goals, work harder, and win more.

The more tools and techniques you master to establish the right mindset, the more you'll find yourself energetic, happy and free.

Part IV:

Strategy Execution for Concentration, Flow and Energy

"Most of what we say and do is not essential. If you can eliminate it, you'll have more time, and more tranquility. Ask yourself at every moment, "Is this necessary?"

Marcus Aurelius

"Are your thoughts worthy of you? If not – NOW is the time to change them. You can begin right where you are right now. Nothing matters but this moment and what you are focusing your attention on."

— **Rhonda Byrne,** bestselling author of *The Secret*

19 Strategies to Maximize Deep Focus

"Knowing is not enough; we must apply.
Willing is not enough; we must do."

Johann Wolfgang von Goethe

So far, this book has equipped you with the background literature on how deep focus can help you, how you can eliminate your blocks and how you can begin to build deep focus.

Additionally, with the help of the quick exercises you've been working with so far, you've started to reflect upon where you truly stand in your journey towards building focus. You've begun to see how some powerful principles can be applied into your day-to-day life.

You've even learnt the benefits of being in a focused flow state and suggestions on how you can go about creating the same for yourself.

This section of the book will now equip you with a set of engaging strategies based on rigorous research, aimed at helping you maximize your concentration, flow, and energy.

Some of these techniques may sound surprising to you, while others might sound simple and obvious. But, each one is powerful in its own way. Some strategies will help you revisit your time-management and help you prioritize better. Yet, other strategies will have you assessing your boundaries and distractions.

And lastly, some will have you take a hard look at how wisely you're expending your mental energy. You might choose to work with strategies that are completely new to you or might choose to fine-tune the ones that you're already applying in your life on some level.

Each person is wired in a unique way, and what works wonders for one may not work so well for another. The idea is for you to browse through each of these strategies, select the ones that suit your lifestyle and goals, and then commit to applying them in your life day after day.

The longer you stick with them, the more your endeavors to build focus will snowball, and the more extraordinary your results will be.

You'll find a small prompt at the end of each strategy to make your notes and to encourage you to immediately begin to apply what you have just learnt.

It's time for execution!

Here's a list of the 19 strategies. You can go through them in sequence or begin by diving into the ones that resonate with you the most. What matters is that you take one strategy and put it into action. You can focus on one strategy a day or commit to one per week.

1. Apply the 2-minute rule
2. Begin with small chunks of hyper-focused work
3. Make it easier for yourself to make decisions
4. Improve your time batching
5. Use 'halfway' breaks
6. Schedule morning power hours
7. Prioritize using the 'ABCDE' method
8. Make a 'not-to-do' list
9. Use music to sharpen your focus
10. Learn when and how to say 'no'
11. Get offline and turn off your phone (no, really)
12. Have an accountability partner
13. Make handy notes when you read

14. Track your small wins
15. Set healthy boundaries
16. Create and stick to a daily routine
17. Get rid of your perfection obsession
18. Assess your selective attention
19. Release your past, visualize your future, and focus on your present

Strategy 1: Apply the 2-Minute Rule

"Every action you take is a vote for the type of person you wish to become. No single instance will transform your beliefs, but as the votes build up, so does the evidence of your new identity."

James Clear, bestselling author of *Atomic Habits*

Many times, you set ambitious goals when you're feeling motivated, and when it comes to execution, you procrastinate or give up altogether. Your mind wanders: perhaps you could do it better if you scheduled the activity for the next week? If this sounds familiar, the 2-minute rule can help you break this pattern.

Published by David Allen in his book titled 'Getting Things Done,' the 2-minute rule, at its essence, mentions that *'if an action you think of will take less than 2 minutes, it should be done at the moment it's defined.'*

The logic is that it will take you longer to further think about it, schedule it and discuss it than it will to immediately complete it. If you struggle with procrastination or find that you've become generally lazy about certain things, this could be a great way to jolt yourself out of the rut.

James Clear, an authority on building great habits, suggests that big or intimidating habits or goals should be broken down into small steps that can be executed easily. The idea is to simply get yourself started *now*, as opposed to planning and delaying a bigger task for later. For instance, if you intend to build the habit of painting for stress-relief, you could focus on execution by taking out your canvas, paints, and brushes immediately.

While these small steps might sound simple, they have three benefits: they get you to immediate action, thus making the next step easier, and the one after that, and they compound over time, helping you affirm a sense of identity. The more you begin to relate with something as a part of your identity, the more it becomes 'you,' as opposed to being just another far-fetched goal.

A focus on immediate execution, even for as little as 2 minutes, keeps you from getting stuck with long-term planning, elaborate decision-making, and fanciful hypothesizing. We've all been guilty of it! While some life-altering or high-stakes decisions certainly do require a great deal of brainstorming and scenario visualization, for most of your day-to-day decisions, you'd probably be a lot further along if you would just *get started*.

The 2-minute rule can help you get things off your plate one-by-one. When you look back at the end of the day, not only would you have completed several small tasks – you would have broken your pattern of procrastination. And the more repetitively you actually do something, the easier it becomes over time, and the more driven you become by seeing your own progress.

And it's all going to start with just 2 minutes.

Call to Action

Note down your thoughts with regards to executing this strategy, and how it can help you. For instance, think about:

Make a list of tasks you can start right now. Choose one task from the list. Set your timer for 2 minutes and begin working on this task. Stop working after 2 minutes. Do you feel like continuing? Do it. Push it to 5 minutes. The point to this exercise is simple: Just begin!

How can this strategy help you in the long term? What immediate steps can you take to execute this strategy?

Strategy 2: Work in Small Chunks of Hyper-Focused Work

"Your purpose in life is to find your purpose and give your whole heart and soul to it."

Buddha

Do you know of anyone who gets so completely lost in their work that nothing can distract them? They don't stop to eat, or to take a break; it seems as though they wouldn't stop what they were doing if an earthquake struck. You might have seen this with a painter, or a scientist, or even someone immersed in a really interesting book.

You might have heard of the term hyper-focus in the context of ADHD (or Attention Deficit Hyperactivity Disorder), but stripped from the negative connotations, hyper focus is simply intense fixation or attention to a task at the cost of all else.

Imagine if you could be intensely focused on one task after another, without getting distracted! In the same way that people with ADHD can harness their hyper focus productively by channeling it towards positive activities, you want to prioritize important work and dive into it head-on and knock it off your to-do list.

A great way to get yourself into the habit of developing deep focus is to break down what you need to do into smaller chunks that you can intensively focus on. While you're committed to the task at hand, avoid all distractions or breaks. Stop only when it's time to stop.

You could set up alarms on your phone or computer to remind you when it's time to get ready for that meeting or to leave to pick up your daughter from school. Until then, reserve all your attention for the one task at hand.

Not only will focusing on small chunks of work help you accomplish what you need to do, it will also help you develop the ability to concentrate on tasks for larger periods of time in the longer run.

Call to Action

Try breaking down all tasks into smaller fragments of time that you can complete in 5-15 minutes or less.

Focus on one small task at a time without any distractions. If you want to track your time, implement the Pomodoro Technique.

Form a habit of adding structure to your tasks by time chunking. Focus on a tiny piece at a time. Progress is made with baby steps, one step at a time.

Strategy 3: Simplify Your Decision-Making Process

"You don't need to see the whole staircase, just take the first step."

Martin Luther King Jr.

Technology and a culture of consumerism ensures that we're constantly flooded with a deluge of options. When you have an absurd number of choices in every aspect of your life and work, it's natural for you to be left feeling overwhelmed now and then.

Think about the last time you made a choice immediately, without hesitation or deliberation. For your last vacation, how easily were you able to decide where to travel to? Or which hotel to stay at? Or even where to go for dinner on your first night there?

With more choices, you're prompted to dig in deeper and do more research. As you get lost in more literature and opinions, you're bogged down. How do you know what's good enough? What if you miss out on something because you didn't plan properly? What if you could have anticipated something in advance and had a better experience? And so goes the trail of choices and decisions.

When this happens frequently enough, maybe you forget to stop and see the problem from a distance. Or perhaps you completely stop trusting your gut. In the worst case, you give up on the task completely.

You can stop yourself from going down this road altogether if you simply make it easy for yourself to make decisions. When you make it easier for yourself to choose, you automatically make it easier for yourself to focus.

Let's say you want to lose weight. What do you need to do to get going? You probably need to eat healthier and exercise more; to do this, go buy your green veggies and make sure you go for a run today. That's it! No need for a whole list of choices or elaborate decision-making.

As soon as you know what you want and why you want it, focus on *getting started*. Trust that you'll make the right decisions along the way. You'll spend a great deal of time and energy in decision fatigue if you let yourself get overwhelmed constantly.

Here are five tips to help you make it easier for you to choose:

1. Hone your intuition and learn to trust it
2. Learn to look at situations from a different perspective
3. Develop systems in your day-to-day life so that you don't spend time making routine decisions, for instance with regards to clothing or food choices
4. Give up the worry of missing out and believe in abundance instead
5. Set deadlines by which you need to make decisions and stick to them

Once you've made your decision, ensure you see it through. Improve your confidence over time by making decisions quickly and trusting yourself more by taking rapid action…even if you're unsure of the decision.

In advance, you can never know the outcome of decisions until you reach the outcome, but one thing is for certain…if you decide nothing, then nothing is what your results will be.

Call to Action

1. Decide on something that you have been avoiding. This could be a decision that changes the way you eat, think, or how you control your behavior. Your decision might be something you have to discuss first with your partner or children.
2. After making this decision, stick with it and follow through with your first course of action.
3. Create a goal for yourself to make one important decision per day and follow through with the first action step.

Strategy 4: Improve Your Time Batching

"Time isn't the main thing; it's the only thing."

Miles Davis

As you go about your day, do you find yourself jumping from one activity to the next? Even if you're completing each activity, do you find yourself doing something very similar to what you did earlier that day?

Maybe you wrote an email in the morning, and at night you're writing out the same content in the brochure you're preparing for marketing. Or maybe you had a performance review session with your analyst last morning and spent all of last evening in a similar meeting with your boss.

It's likely that different areas of your work require different skills sets, a different kind of focus, or even different levels of immersion on your part. For some tasks you may need to concentrate in seclusion, for others you may need to listen to several points of view simultaneously. Here's where time batching can help you.

Batching together related tasks (or tasks that require similar effort on your part) for a specific period can make it easier for you to focus, before moving on to a different set of tasks. You're probably already applying time batching in your day-to-day life, without realizing it. For example, at home, you wouldn't do two of the dishes, go to lay out your clothes for the next day, return to do three more dishes, and then go back to pick out your accessories, would you?

You'd finish doing the dishes, and then lay out your outfit (and maybe pick the one for the day after as well, since you're already at it). But it's likely that you're not following time batching at work.

Let's say you finished one client meeting, and you take a quick look at your emails. You're almost done with one report, but the next one will have to wait because you're getting into a performance review session. Sound familiar?

What if, instead, you decide to check and write all your emails together. You could schedule one day on your calendar just for updates from each of your analysts or managers. You could block out a couple of hours to write out one report after another. Or you could club your client meetings together, wherever possible. Naturally, you may want to prioritize tasks requiring more concentration before the ones that require lower energy.

Time batching helps boost productivity by encouraging deeper focus and limiting distractions. It helps prevent constant interruptions to your workflow.

Applied firm-wide, and in synchronization between colleagues wherever possible, time batching could improve productivity for the whole team. Time batching ensures you're not repeating similar tasks in a scattered manner at different instances. It reduces the number of errors you make and keeps you from multi-tasking. Cumulatively, it can certainly help your work move more seamlessly, reducing your levels of stress and anxiety.

So, leave all those twitter and Instagram updates for the end of the day!

Call to Action

By following some of the best practices around time batching, you can improve productivity and focus.

1. Group your tasks by function and/or objective, and then assign each to a set window of time. For example, 8:00-9:00 a.m. might be the time block that you respond to social media comments and questions, but for the rest of the day, your Facebook and Instagram access is restricted.

2. Enter your batched tasks into a calendar or scheduling tool so you have a visual representation of how you'll spend your time during the week, day by day. Be mindful of how you schedule things–if you frequently have meetings or calls on a certain day, you may structure things differently on those days.

3. Set reminders or alerts that keep you on track with the set blocks of times you've established for task-related work. Over time, you might delete these reminders.

4. Turn your devices to Do Not Disturb mode and close your open tabs to eliminate distractions. Close the door to your workspace and/or put on headphones to eliminate noise.

Strategy 5: Use 'halfway' Breaks

"It's the energy you expend, not the time you spend."

Tony Schwartz

In the same manner that you're working on managing your time better, it's important for you to manage your energy better. Taking a pause in the middle of your day to recharge and refuel can prevent you from burning out as you go along your day.

There are many ways in which you could use your daily 'halfway' break – you could catch up with a friend over lunch, turn off your phone and go for a walk, or even exercise and meditate for a total of 30-40 minutes.

Managing your energy and chalking out times for taking breaks has become even more important in working from home. With personal and professional spaces blurred, it's harder to stick to a schedule with clear hours for work and separate ones for play.

When you can't separate where you work from where you unwind, scheduling and sticking to your break so that you're taking a breather becomes even more important.

In scheduling your halfway break, consider your natural productivity patterns, so that you're not interfering with the time periods in which you do your best work. It's a good idea to listen to your body.

For instance, do you find you develop a headache if you continuously look at your computer screen for several hours at a stretch? You might want to schedule a break session to get up and move around.

Do you feel refreshed after a 40-minute yoga session in the afternoon? Use it to unwind and go back to your work energized for the rest of the day.

Make sure that you choose activities that really help you unwind during your break. For instance, you may not want to catch up with your lawyer over an intense conversation or plan to read a difficult report. The whole idea is to rejuvenate and unwind, even if it's just for a short while, so that you can go about your day with more energy. You should be able to be completely present in your activities once you've resumed your work after your break.

One of the challenging aspects of executing halfway breaks might be establishing boundaries with your managers or colleagues. You want to push yourself and have the conversations you need to; get them to see how scheduling your halfway breaks is boosting your energy and productivity. As with anything else, this first step may appear to be the hardest, but once you've taken it, you'll benefit from it for a long time to come.

Call to Action

Schedule in your halfway breaks throughout the day. You can use this brief time to **connect with your mind** for ten minutes, listen to **white noise** (yes, this has benefits for the brain in small doses), or power up with an energy drink.

Your halfway break is to be used for reenergization.

Avoid checking email, scrolling through phone messages or social media, and any activity detrimental to relaxing your mind.

Strategy 6: Schedule Your Morning Power Hour

"Wake up early and tackle the day before it tackles you. Be on the offense, and not the defense."

Evan Carmichael

The advice of waking up early and using your morning wisely is age-old and well-established. Modern day productivity experts such as Tim Ferriss to Robin Sharma echo these thoughts and provide precise roadmaps for scheduling your mornings (specifically, the first one hour) to gear up as best as you can to tackle your day.

The main idea of using a morning 'power hour' is to get a head-start on the day, and to wire your mind for stability. When you start your day well, you feel like you're in control. You're more likely to retain focus and maintain composure throughout the rest of your day, no matter what comes up as you go along.

Robin Sharma, in his book titled the 5 AM club, advocates a 20/20/20 framework, which suggests breaking up the first hour of your morning into three parts of 20 minutes each, for physical exercise, journaling / meditation and learning respectively.

Tim Ferriss, a widely read author on productivity also mentions that, he personally follows a similar approach. He meditates for the first 20 minutes of his morning hour, and then sits down to journal, followed by rigorous exercise such as biking or high-intensity interval training.

Exercising the first thing in the morning is a fantastic way to start the day. The release of a rush of endorphins, serotonin, and dopamine elevates your levels of optimism and happiness. You could practice yoga to stretch yourself or go for a run.

More and more people are beginning to see the benefits of journaling in the morning as well; it helps you get your thoughts out on paper so that your mind is clear for the rest of the day.

It nudges you to articulate your dominant thoughts and ideas. A wonderful practice in journaling is to write down what you're grateful for each morning, which helps you start the day on a note of positivity. Lastly, learning something new each morning can work wonders in your long-term personal growth.

You could read a chapter from a book, listen to a podcast, or dive into your favorite magazine. You could even enroll in an academic course online and watch a short lecture. If you were to commit time to learn every single day, month after month, year after year, imagine the leaps you'd make!

It might be hard to get into a morning routine if you're not used to one, but your heightened focus levels during the day lead to greater clarity, creativity and a greater sense of awareness.

Call to Action

Here is an example of a **bulletproof morning routine**. This is the same routine practiced by Tom Bilyeu, CEO and Founder of the hit show *Impact Theory*:

Your morning power hour begins with preparing in the evening.

Before bed, lay out your gym/exercise gear. Include your headphones for meditative music or listening to a podcast.

- Wake up 5am (out of bed by 5:05)
- Drink a Glass of water
- Stretch/workout (10 minutes)
- Meditate (10 minutes) Note: I use the **Silva Method** formula
- Read for 20 minutes
- Write down your goals for the day (5 minutes)
- Review your Big Vision (5 minutes)

Strategy 7: Prioritize Tasks with the 'ABCDE' Method

"Things which matter most must never be at the mercy of things which matter least."

Johann Wolfgang von Goethe

This strategy will provide you with a solid technique for time management; the ABCDE method is about prioritizing your work! The 'ABCDE' technique specifically teaches you how to categorize all the items on your to-do list into five categories:

According to productivity expert **Brian Tracy**:

"The ABCDE Method is a powerful priority setting technique that you can use every single day. This technique is so simple and effective that it can, all by itself, make you one of the most efficient and effective people in your field."

This is a breakdown of the **ABCDE** Method:

A: These items are the most important and go right at the top of your list. Note: *If you have more than one A task, you prioritize these tasks by writing "A-1," "A-2," "A-3," and so on in front of each task.*

B: These are items that are important as well but aren't as consequential as those in category A. *Note: The rule is that you should never do a B task when an A task is left undone.*

C: These are tasks that you need to get around to, but have no immediate consequences if postponed

D: These are tasks that you can delegate, thus freeing up your time for 'A' and 'B' tasks

E: These are tasks you should delete from your list altogether

The idea is, you must finish your 'A' tasks before the 'B' ones, and the 'B' ones before the 'C' ones.

Here is how you can apply the ABCDE method to assign priority to each specific task:

(1). Write down all your tasks that must be done for the next day. Note: You can actually do this for the week and then break it down into daily tasks.

You then place an A, B, C, D, or E next to each item on your list before you begin the first task. Refer to the list above.

While following such a system of categorization might seem time consuming at first, it prompts you to articulate what's the most important on your list…and what's not. By separating your level of priorities, you can optimize your efficiency; it ensures you spend your time focusing on the critical tasks that align with your goals for that day, month and year.

Knowing that you're on top of the most important things and are delegating or even striking off things you don't need to do by yourself can save you much time, boost your energy, and relieve you of a great deal of stress.

Call to Action

(1). Create a list of your tasks for this week (or the following week). Now use the ABCDE method to delegate priority to each task.

(2). Block in time on Sunday for 30 minutes to identify priority tasks for the following week. You can write down your tasks in a journal or weekly scheduler.

Strategy 8: Make a 'things-not-to-do' List

"Deciding what not to do is as important as deciding what to do."

Steve Jobs

Do you make a 'to-do' list every day? Even though you do your best to stick to it, do you find that there are days on which you can't get anything ticked off? What if you could flip it around?

A great idea to break the pattern of struggling to stay on top of your list of things to do is to make a list of things *not* to do. These are things that distract you and take away your precious time. They force you to find ways to bring yourself back to focusing on the task at hand, again and again.

Here are some things that could be on your 'not-to-do' list:

- Getting onto Facebook during work hours
- Spending a lot of time on television series or movies during weekdays
- Scheduling longer periods of time for things that could be just as effective with shorter, more intensive sessions, such as exercising
- Logging onto streaming services such as YouTube while at work
- Spending a lot of time on things that could be accomplished more effectively, such as going out to pick up your coffee versus making one at home or in the office
- Wasting time while commuting

A 'not-to-do' list will show you how much time you're wasting away each day or week that you could use productively instead. It can make you cognizant of just how much you're missing out on.

Your time is precious, and you want to focus on what truly matters most, setting yourself up for optimum energy and focus.

Call to Action

- For the next five minutes, **create your list of things not-to-do**. This brings awareness to these activities the moment you start doing them. My #1 thing is **no checking email** during workflow time.
- Make a note of the five things you tend to do that interrupt focus and flow time.
- Focus on breaking this habit when you are tempted to interrupt your focused flow for a distraction.

Strategy 9: Use Music to Sharpen Focus

"Always remember, your focus determines your reality."

George Lucas

Studies on music—and its effect on the brain—have shown that the kind of music you listen to can either stimulate your mental activity or act as a sedative. Music can help you shift your mood, control your emotions, inspire you to action, embolden you, relieve stress, and even help you improve muscle memory.

Certain kinds of music can act as a wonderful tool to sharpen focus; it's proven to help athletes and scientists alike. Here's why listening to music can help sharpen your focus and concentration:

- Music activates the entire brain, lighting up several areas responsible for functions as diverse as regulating stress and motor performance to maintaining rhythm.
- Music can help with the secretion of dopamine, which boosts emotions of positivity and lessens emotions of pain.
- Upbeat music encourages activities such as high intensity workouts, whereas ambient music can stimulate calmness for practices such as yoga.

While some people argue that they find music distracting, others swear that certain kinds of music help them focus, meditate, or study much better.

This is because we are always operating on **two levels**.

Our conscious mind is the one we steer towards the things we want to focus on and accomplish, and our unconscious attention system processes things that are happening all around us, whether we consciously realize it or not.

That's why you may find yourself distracted from the task at hand time and again. It's possible that music helps put this unconscious attention system to work by enabling it to focus on the music, thereby reducing your distractions.

According to a 2007 study from the Stanford University School of Medicine, classical music can help your brain absorb and interpret new information more easily. Your brain processes the abundance of information it receives from the world around you by separating it into smaller segments.

The researchers found evidence to suggest that music can engage your brain in such a way that it trains it to pay better attention to events and make predictions about what might happen.

Listening to classical music can help older adults perform better on memory and processing certain tasks.

Music helps stimulate your brain, similar to the way exercise helps stimulate your body.

You want to stick to music that you like and that elevates and soothes you for better focus, as opposed to music that negatively impacts your emotions, or contains loud, distracting lyrics.

Call to Action

Create a playlist of music you can access right away for the various tasks you perform throughout the day. For my workouts, I use music that is fast paced and energetic. For writing or meditation, ambience tunes or classical music enhance focus and creativity.

I recommend the track weightless by Marconi Union. Its carefully arranged harmonies, rhythms, and bass lines help slow a listener's heart rate, reduce blood pressure and, in addition, lower levels of the stress hormone cortisol.

Strategy 10: Learn When and How to Say *No*

"The difference between successful people and very successful people is that very successful people say no to almost everything."

Warren Buffett

It's possible that you know that saying 'no' is just as important as saying 'yes' when it comes to focusing for success in any endeavor. No one can (or should) do *everything*. You need to concentrate on some things, which means you need to say no to other things. You need to focus on things that move you towards your goals, without getting pulled into the things that keep you from your goals.

The biggest minds in the world, from Steve Jobs to Warren Buffett, have advocated the practice of eliminating and relentlessly saying no to all things that are not truly essential. It's necessary for productivity, it's important for focus, and it's invaluable for success. List out what's truly important, what really matters, and say no to all the rest, and you're naturally freeing up time and space to focus better!

The problem, however, is that saying 'no' is hard. What if you offend someone? How can you say no to your favorite colleague, your best friend, or your boss? What if you're perceived as unhelpful? What if you need their help subsequently?

There are many thoughts on similar lines that might be keeping you from confidently saying no in your day-to-day life. This in turn may be leading you to give in to distractions at the cost of your focus.

Here are some suggestions to get you more comfortable with the practice of saying no:

Practice being polite but be direct. Explain (briefly) why you're saying no, but say no clearly, without beating around the bush

Take charge and offer help in a manner that suits you

Understand when someone is genuinely asking for help, and when someone is manipulating you and address the requests appropriately

Build confidence in yourself. Understand your responsibilities and your roles well, and then set boundaries firmly

Accommodate the request if it's feasible, but without getting burdened – feel free to ask follow-up questions to arrive at a win-win solution

Don't feel guilty. Understand that taking on more than you can handle is detrimental to everyone in the long run

Always remember that no one can do all things all the time or be everything to everyone. Saying no is a crucial, if difficult, necessity from time to time, and learning how to say no gracefully can help you a great deal in your journey towards success.

Call to Action

Be firm with your NO. If you know with certainty the answer is a definitive no, don't drag it out by saying maybe–or even "yes"– without an intention of following through. You will be saving people the stress of waiting or guessing if you're ever going to come through for them. **If you aren't planning to take action on the requested task, let the other person know on the spot so you can both move on.**

Don't Overcommit. You have to know what your priorities are. You can't commit to everything. If you do, you end up with a stressful situation that you now have to manage. Doing favors and helping people is important, but not at the expense of your own loss if you try to "people-please" everybody.

Strategy 11: Get Offline and Turn Off Your Phone

"To do two things at once is to do neither."

Publilius Syrus

In some cases, your distractions may come about from things that are not in your control. In most cases however, you can control your distraction triggers. One of your biggest distractions triggers is your phone!

While you might argue that it's not feasible for you to turn off your phone all day, you could put it on airplane mode or 'do-not-disturb' mode for those few hours in which you need to intensely concentrate.

When you're not constantly checking your messages, photos, social media updates or emails, you're much more likely to dive deeper into the task at hand, whether it's a professional or personal one. Your mind will know that you're committed entirely to the activity in front of you, and that you won't entertain any meandering. You'll be present more fully, more acutely aware of your situation, processing important and relevant information much better.

Besides getting off your phone, unplugging from the internet, whether it be for a couple of hours or couple of weeks, can also boost your energy substantially. Zoning out, zooming out and adopting an entirely different viewpoint are all wonderful ways to help you break an unhelpful pattern or chain of thoughts, or even allow you to solve a problem better.

But to do this successfully, you need to completely stop what you're doing; and almost everything we do is usually connected to the internet.

Here are eleven activities you could try to do while you're spending time offline:

1. Cook a delicious meal with a family member or friend

2. Immerse yourself fully into any activity you love, whether its painting or brewing your favorite coffee

3. Go for a run, or take your dog for a walk

4. Book a digital detox yoga retreat or silent meditation retreat

5. Go and explore your city. Remember how you got by before Google maps!

6. Practice a stress-relieving yoga pose called 'Viparita Karani' or 'Legs Up the Wall', where you simply lay down on your back and prop your legs straight up 90 degrees against a wall. You'll feel your tension melt away.

7. Read (and disappear into) a novel by your favorite author

8. Handwrite notes. When was the last time you wrote a heartfelt thank you note to someone?

9. Pamper yourself with a luxurious bath

10. Go for a picnic in the park, or walk around a gallery

11. Simply take a nap

Unplugging or having a digital detox can help you boost your productivity, energy and focus substantially, especially if integrated into a routine and practiced over time. You'll begin to thoroughly enjoy it and see the benefits to your mind and life accumulate.

Call to Action

Make your own expanded list of activities to do offline. You can test your ideas to discover the tasks that work best with your mood and creativity. You could learn a new skill or figure out a new way to build a second income stream.

Strategy 12: Connect with an Accountability Partner

*"Alone we can do so little.
Together we can do so much."*

Helen Keller

All of us need a little push now and then, and while our family and friends are usually around, it might not always be the case. You might be living or working abroad, or you might want to work on your goals without involving them.

In such cases, an accountability partner can help you stay on track and maintain focus.

Think of an accountability partner as a coach who you will help in return, with each of you pushing the other to accomplish your goals. People have accountability partners in areas of life where they generally require a bit of a nudge, such as going for that early morning run, or joining a challenging book club.

Whatever you choose to do, whether it's meditating to build mindfulness or following a healthy diet, an accountability partner can help you stay the course.

You want to make sure you choose a partner you're compatible with and that your schedules align. It should ideally be someone you respect as you're more likely to stick to working towards your goals if you both take each other seriously.

A great accountability partner will encourage you to be honest with yourself, to set and achieve realistic and yet 'stretch' goals, keep you inspired, help you review progress, and finally, celebrate your wins with you!

If you don't have a colleague, family member or friend in mind for an accountability partner, you could find an accountability partner virtually or via an app. This concept is a helpful one globally, and many people around the world are using the accountability system to stay productive and achieve amazing results.

Call to Action

You can find an accountability partner through mastermind groups or via apps that connect you with accountability groups or coaches. Remember that your accountability partner is someone who can help you, and you can help them. It must be a win-win situation, or it won't work.

Strategy 13: Make Easy-to-Reference Notes When You Read

"Simplicity is a choice, a discrimination, a crystallization. Its object is purity."

Le Corbusier

You're right in the middle of an important task, and you need to refer to something you recently read that might help you with it. You know it was somewhere in this book, or on that particular website, but you can't seem to find it, and you've broken your chain of thought. Sound familiar?

Reading is great to build your knowledge database, but you do need to have a clear referencing system so that you can refer to the right literature while maintaining your focus.

This could be as simple as highlighting parts of your favorite books (you could color code your highlights). You could use bookmarks on your laptop, or apps such as OneNote or Evernote, using tags to find what you're looking for more easily. Highlighting or noting down excerpts you feel will help you later lets you quickly refer to parts of a text that matter, in a timely and convenient manner.

Some readers like to make bullet points on the margins of the books as they read. Others like to summarize each chapter at the end. Use whatever technique helps you focus best while reading, as well as makes for a convenient reference system.

Here are three simple strategies for focusing on the content as well as improving your memory:

1. Use sticky notes. When you come across a tactic or information with the intent of using it later, write it down on a sticky (paste it) note. Tack it to the back of the book or a space on your wall.
2. Highlight the important points for easy reference. For as long back as I can remember, I have always read books with a yellow highlighter. Later, when I wanted to reference a certain point, it

was easy to find. Highlighting also helps to retain the information as it draws in your brain's focus on that information.

Call to Action

Develop your own system for taking notes and easy-referencing the material you read. This works for fiction or nonfiction. It works for textbooks or digital material. If you read with e-books, there is a highlighting function built into the software, and you can bookmark the pages, too.

Strategy 14: Track Your Small Wins

"The journey of a thousand miles begins with a single step."

Lao Tzu

In his book 'Atomic Habits', author James Clear posits that even a 1% improvement in any activity every day for a year results in a cumulative improvement of 37 times by the end of the year.

It's easy to underestimate the snowballing effect of small steps taken day after day. We're so used to getting enthralled with the overnight successes and big wins, that we forget that everything starts with that first small step.

Sharpening your mind, improving your ability to focus, and developing more mental energy is a difficult process requiring a lot of continuous effort. It's easy to give up on something when you don't see a big difference right away, or in the first few days. That's why it's important to track small wins, and to remind yourself that you are indeed progressing, step by step.

Tracking your small wins keeps you engaged, excited, and invested in the activities that lead you to your big goals, making it easier for you to focus on them better.

You want to celebrate your small wins as often as you can to amplify the feeling of joy and positivity, and you need to let your small losses go, trusting that you'll progress.

Small wins compounded over time lead to bigger wins. An example of a small win would be cleaning one room in your house and not the entire house. Or, losing one pound per week on a diet instead of focusing on twenty pounds to lose over the next three months. One reason you allow procrastination to take over is your fixation on the big win that requires lots of work and a dedicated time block.

Constantly ask yourself, "What is the next immediate step I can take to keep moving forward." Then, take that step. Whatever it takes to hit your big goal, you can always begin with the absolute minimum step necessary.

It could take weeks or months to finish an extensive project, but when you count the small wins, it builds momentum faster.

Start with small steps and build momentum. Soon, your consistent actions will reveal what you can accomplish when you take small steps consistently.

Here are four simple steps you can take right now:

1. Write down your #1 goal for this year. If this is overwhelming, what is your goal for the next thirty days? You want to take intentional action towards this goal, even if it is an action that takes you less than 2 minutes to do.

2. For the next five minutes, make a list of all the small, manageable action steps related to this goal. Write everything down. Is it an email you have to send or an app you have to download? Is it a chapter in a book you should read?

3. Build up your momentum over the weeks and months ahead. Looking back six months from now, you'll feel like a mountaineer, looking down from the mountain you have just ascended… one step at a time.

4. Now, take the simplest step possible on your list. Do this task right now.

Call to Action

Keep a journal of your small wins. Every day you can make a note of the small tasks you completed. Imagine where you'll be one month, three months, and one year from now.

Strategy 15: Set Healthy Boundaries

"Boundaries define what is me and what is not me. A boundary shows me where I end and someone else begins, leading me to a sense of ownership. Knowing what I am gives me freedom."

Henry Cloud, author of *Boundaries*

An extremely important strategy to help you improve your focus is to establish and adhere to boundaries with the people around you. To many people, setting boundaries might seem to be a negative or rude idea, but it is, in fact, necessary for your wellbeing.

By setting healthy boundaries you're simply taking care of yourself. You're allowing for the creation of a zone in which you can work or think uninterrupted, thus preventing unnecessary disturbances, annoyances, delays, frustrations, and anger.

Setting boundaries does not mean you're avoiding people, becoming detached or spoiling your relationships; it means you're learning to say 'no' when you need to, prioritizing your work, preventing oversharing, and not doing things simply because you want to please others.

Ideally, for maximum focus and growth, you should set healthy boundaries across several areas of your life. These could be physical boundaries (such as keeping an office cabin or cubicle) or intellectual boundaries (wherein you discuss certain ideas with more like-minded people).

They could also be emotional boundaries with colleagues or friends, or financial ones (for instance, you may not like to loan money to family members to prevent relationships from going sour in case of non-repayment).

To successfully set and maintain boundaries, make sure you set reasonable ones, be consistent in keeping them, and communicate with respect.

As you set your boundaries and work on your journey of personal growth, you must also remember to respect those of others. Learn how to listen when others say no, ensure you value their perceptions, and understand their needs just as you'd like them to do for you.

Call to Action

Write down one area in your life that requires healthy boundaries. Is it in a relationship? A work situation? Or do you need to set boundaries with yourself?

Next, identify the reasons you struggle to set boundaries. Is it fear of repercussion? You might upset someone? The fear of isolating yourself?

There are many reasons we fail to set boundaries. By discovering why, you don't set them empowers you to be more diligent in doing it.

Strategy 16: Create (and Stick to) a Daily Routine

"Don't be fooled by the calendar. There are only as many days in the year as you make use of. One man gets only a week's value out of a year, while another gets a full year's value out of a week."

Charles Richards

You know by now that success is as much about consistent execution as it is about goal-setting and intentions. Execution is why you need a personalized daily routine. You need to figure out what to do, how to do it, and when to do it.

As you've learnt with several other strategies here, you want to go with the pattern and flow that works best for your life and work styles.

Are you an early riser? Schedule your **hardest tasks** for the morning, when your focus is at its peak. Typically, by mid-day, you're likely to have lost some of your morning steam, so you could plan to use these hours to do more routine tasks that don't require a lot of brainpower.

Do you work best at night with the rest of the world asleep? Plan hard tasks for the night. And as you build your daily routine, it might be wise to factor in break-times and downtimes because you must step back and pause every now and then. Schedule time for that meditation or a quick run.

No matter what routine you design for yourself, it's important to stick to it day after day, allowing your body and mind to assimilate it and get into a flow.

Test your routine - try it out for a few days, change what doesn't work, and come up with what works best and lets you perform at your optimum level of concentration.

A carefully thought-through system helps keep you in control of your day, instead of your day getting the better of you!

Here are several strategies you can begin implementing from today to build better structure into your routine and workflow:

Track your work: One of the most difficult challenges with time control is knowing what you're working on. But effective time control begins with knowing where you are putting your time. This is a highly disciplined habit where you are literally writing down what you are working on and how long was spent on this task. This gives you an optimal view of how you spend your time.

Set up 30-minute time blocks. No interruptions. Work through the time and train your mind to stay fixed on the work that is in front of you. This means closing all other tabs. Take breaks but keep it limited, and use that time for breathing or stretching, if you're sitting down for long periods of time.

Do the hard things first. Take the three tasks you are focused on and tackle the one thing that causes you most resistance. That is where you start your day.

Eliminate the nonessential. Track with a pen and paper pad. I use a pen and paper to write down what I'm working on as I'm working on it. Not a digital tracker although there are plenty. Why? Optimization begins with elimination of the nonessential tools and distractors.

Write down all the tasks that make up your daily routine. Are there any new tasks that need to be implemented to make your routine more efficient? Is there an area where you can save time by spending less time doing it? Get into the habit of writing down the tasks you do as you start working.

Call to Action

Daily Review Session: The best time of day is when you run through a checklist of what you did well and what you didn't get to or failed to achieve. Were you distracted or had negative thoughts that took control of your day? Do a daily review session for 15 minutes.

Strategy 17: Get Rid of Your Obsession with Perfection

"Have no fear of perfection - you'll never reach it."

Salvador Dali

If you're a perfectionist, or are heavily influenced by one, be it your boss, parent or friend, it could be negatively impacting your ability to focus and get things done more than you can immediately imagine.

If you're obsessed with things being absolutely perfect, are unable to share your work unless it's 100% right, or approve of a piece of work unless its 'flawless', you might not be able to get things off your plate. In extreme cases, the need for perfectionism may even prevent you from beginning at all!

A fear of not being perfect leads to stress, creates nervousness and frustration, and seriously affects your relationships with the people working or living with you. Be honest with yourself. Your perfectionism is probably standing in the way of your work, or causing you undue stress.

If you're like most people who deal with perfectionistic tendencies, you work hard and keep pushing yourself until it's just right. But the challenge with perfection is, it's extremely difficult to actually finish anything. You continue to *tweak it* here and there, making just one more change, one final stroke of the pen, or another slight adjustment to the right until your high standards have been met.

Then, you start all over again. Perfection takes daily focus to manage. Building awareness into your life and work will help you to move forward and make progress.

Here are some suggestions to help you deal with it.

1. Realize that it's great to set and achieve high standards, and not always necessary to hit the 'perfect' mark
2. Accept that no one can always control everything and that everyone must adapt

3. Practice voicing your opinion and expressing your perspectives boldly

4. Understand that doing something well is better than not doing it at all out of a fear of failure or disappointment

5. Accept that failing is human, and is in fact, a part of success

6. Learn to slow down, to pause and to relax

7. Realize that *people* are more important than events or deliverables

8. Learn to trust yourself more

Learn to let go of others' approval, learn to love yourself, and to invest in self-care

If you truly care about what you do, it will come through in your sincerity, endeavours and work ethic; don't let the fear of not being perfect keep you from losing your focus.

Call to Action

What is an area of your life that you struggle to make just right? Is it your finances? Your relationships? Your art? Perfection interferes with focus because the perfection becomes the object of your focus.

Brainstorm your ideas from what you have learned in this book to start tackling your obsession with perfection…and we are all obsessed to some degree with doing things perfectly.

Strategy 18: Assess Your Selective Attention

"I am not absentminded. It is the presence of mind that makes me unaware of everything else."

G.K. Chesterton

Our brains are wired for selective attention; we choose what to focus on for a certain period of time and what to ignore. For example, think about the quantum of information you're exposing yourself to every time you step out of your house. There's a noisy intersection, an ice-cream vendor trying to get your attention, a traffic signal turning red, people shouting from across the street, an ambulance racing to an accident scene in the distance, and countless other things going on simultaneously.

Do you notice all of this? No, you probably just saw your friend standing across the street waving at you, and the pedestrian crossing for you to get to her. It isn't possible for you to process and focus on all things at once, so you choose what to concentrate on.

That's selective attention. It works for the things you see, the sounds you hear, and even the memories you hold onto.

In your journey of developing more focus, it might be a good idea to pause and identify what all you're actually paying attention to, and what you're missing out on.

Are there important things at your workplace you could focus on, instead of some of the things you currently do? Where could you improve your productivity? What activities could you eliminate? What do you spend your time on at home? Where else could your mental energy be better used?

Your time and attention are limited, precious resources, and you want to channel how you manage these to build your best self. You want to be a person who operates with clarity and a sense of purpose.

You don't have to notice or pay attention to all the things happening around you. Rather, be selective with what you choose to focus on, and the focused mind you seek will adapt to your desire.

Call to Action

You can improve selective attention by measuring the results you get through repetitive action. If you shoot ten thousand hoops, how has your form, performance and strategy improved from those first few shots? You improve selective attention through practicing one skill over a long duration, and figuring out what works and what doesn't.

When you measure results and test, it increases confidence and you're more likely to repeat that same action to improve results by scaling up.

Selective attention comes down to this:

- Practice one skill
- Measure results and realign
- Continue to improve and repeat

Strategy 19: Release Your Past, Visualize Your Future, and Focus on Your Present

"Forget past mistakes. Forget failures. Forget everything except what you're going to do now and do it."

William Durant, Co-founder of *General Motors*

Being in a state of mindfulness, completely present within the moment in front of you is hard! Your mind races to the future, hypothesizing one scenario after another. Or it goes back suddenly into the past, triggered by something you see or hear. Sometimes it even moves laterally, distracted towards something else that's calling for your attention. And in this manner, you lose out on moment after moment without being present at all.

Learning to be mindful, to be aware, to be completely present, is a powerful weapon and brings you an unparalleled level of focus. A very small percentage of people are fully present in any given instant.

On one hand, visualizing your future is obviously important – you've got to know what dreams and goals you are working towards. But dwelling on the future, or being lost in your dreams, at the cost of the actions you should be taking in the present may be keeping you from progressing.

Thinking too much about the future also leads to unnecessary worry; you might fret over things that might never even happen.

On the other hand, you might be struggling with letting go of your past, which might be keeping you from focussing fully in the present. Recurring negative or toxic thoughts might be replaying in your mind over and over, creating a ceaseless chatter.

Pain from difficult past memories can derail you from your present, or even paralyse you completely, pulling you into a spiral of negativity.

Here are a few ways to pause and release the past (or fear of the future) when you feel overwhelmed:

1. Reframe how you see the situation, for instance, instead of thinking "Why did this have to happen just to me" flip it around as "I'm lucky I got to explore this unique path!"

2. Distance yourself from the past, physically and digitally.

3. Take ownership and understand that your life is your responsibility.

4. Practice deep breathing when you begin to feel uncomfortable or distracted.

5. Be patient. Remind yourself that life is abundant and is teeming with more possibilities than you can currently imagine.

6. Truly learn from your past so that you don't repeat your mistakes, and then let it go.

7. Share your thoughts and concerns with people you trust.

8. Be kind to yourself. Realize that you are trying to do your best to heal and grow.

To unleash your best self and to operate at maximum energy and focus, you need to consciously work on completely releasing the past and the worries of the future and learn to live in the *now*.

Call to Action

When you are feeling moments of confusion, worry or lose your sense of direction, remember the steps mentioned. Write them down in point form:

- Reframe your thoughts about the situation
- Distance yourself
- Take total ownership for your life
- Practice deep breathing
- Be patient. Opportunity is coming your way!
- Learn from your past and remember
- Communicate your emotions with people surrounding you
- Heal and grow from the experience.

Part V:

Feed Your Focus

"Besides the noble art of getting things done, there is the noble art of leaving things undone. The wisdom of life consists in the elimination of non-essentials."

Lin Yutang

Using 'Focus Fuel' to Feed Deep Focus (and keep going)

"Success isn't always about greatness. It's about consistency. Consistent hard work leads to success. Greatness will come."

Dwayne Johnson, "The Rock"

Let's say you've figured out the perfect strategies and set up processes that gear you up to build optimum focus. You've gotten started and you're well on your way to improving your concentration. You're excited about setting yourself up for the best life and the most success you can envision.

Building focus will require more than your motivation and attention; it will require *continuous* energy and effort. Just like you need to provide gas to a car for it to keep running, you need to provide fuel into this (or any) endeavor, so that you keep on going.

This section of the book will show you exactly how to do that, by providing **five mechanisms** that act as focus 'fuel'. We've touched upon these multiple times in the book so far; now you'll learn more about exactly why they're important, how they feed your focus and level your energy, and how you can use them to keep yourself on track.

Each mechanism is important, and each one ties into the others. The more fuel you give yourself, and the better you feed this obsession, the more rapid your growth acceleration will be!

Here are five excellent ways to fuel your focus:

Focus Fuel Method 1: Optimize your 'focus environment' and create your 'focus dome'

In doing everything you can to improve your focus, and while pushing yourself to your outermost limits, you don't want to overlook the impact your environment has on you. Your environment should be working *for* you and should be *helping* you, instead of working *against* you and *costing* you time and energy.

Think of the perfect environment that directs you to focus better—this is your 'focus dome'. You want to set up the optimum surroundings in your focus dome, so that your distractions are controlled, and you can work in deep focus. Your environment can either set you up for success or for failure, so make sure you choose carefully.

Working in a cluttered, disorganized, noisy, or uncomfortable office environment, or working from home in similar conditions, will result in a slower pace of work, increasing stress, and ultimately, leading to less fulfillment in most areas of your life.

You want your environment to be designed such that it is dedicated towards helping you sustain long-term focus. To do this, you must design your lifestyle and your **focus dome** in such a manner that, whenever you need to focus, you are supported to enter a state of flow and concentration.

Here are some suggestions to get you started on building your ideal focus dome:

1. Organize your work environment. Have your drawers and digital folders slotted, clearly label your paper and digital files, classify confidential information correctly, etc.

2. Declutter your spaces, both at work and at home. You could start by removing one unnecessary item each day. Set up an empty box in your space and during the day, drop 'clutter items' into the box for disposal at the end of day.

3. Pin up positive quotes and affirmations on your work-desk, laptop or phone for enhancing motivation and energy levels.

4. Ensure you clean your spaces regularly, including your desks, equipment, work chair, and flooring.

5. Remove distraction triggers. Start the day by turning off notifications on your phone and tablet.

6. Go paperless, go digital! Use cloud storage services such as Google docs or iCloud to open up the physical space in your office.

7. Ensure you choose an ergonomic work chair and have a well-designed work environment with adequate lighting. Comfort matters a great deal when you're spending most of your day there.

8. Have a neat and convenient system to encourage and capture ideas. Use whiteboards, voice recorders, or apps on your phone or tablet.

Focus Fuel Method 2: Get enough sleep everyday

We all know that getting enough sleep is important, but in the rush of things or stress of work, we unconsciously ignore the need to stick to a healthy sleep routine. Sleep is important for your learning as well as your memory. Inadequate sleep makes it harder for you to concentrate, while enough sleep lets your brain unwind and rewire itself so you're ready to tackle the next day with determined enthusiasm.

Here are a few more reasons why it's absolutely necessary for you to get enough sleep:

- **Sleep affects your mood.** When you sleep, your subconscious mind is working on processing your emotions; a lack of sleep is known to impact positive emotions negatively. Regular lack of sleep over a period of time is shown to induce mood disorders, and insomnia can contribute to anxiety and depression.

- **Sleep impacts mental and physical energy.** Adequate sleep allows for muscle recovery and repair, and improves your energy levels. With lack of sleep, exercise during a long day gets harder, compounding the limitations to reaching your maximum level of focus.

- **Sleep affects several other aspects of your overall health,** ranging from your metabolism and heart health to body weight and immune system.

So, leaving aside unforeseen events and circumstances, ensure you stick to a healthy sleep pattern and prepare for at least 6-8 hours of sleep each night.

Many people find short 20-minute power naps to be extremely beneficial. A short afternoon nap can help you feel refreshed and more energetic to carry on the rest of the day. Other benefits include lower fatigue, better vigilance, lower blood pressure, more positive energy and better composure. Remember to stick to short naps of 20-30 minutes, as longer naps could negatively impact your night sleep pattern.

Focus Fuel Method 3: Eat right and begin your day with a healthy meal

If you want your mind and body to function like a well-oiled machine, you've got to feed it with the right fuel.

You want to consume foods that set you up for a day-long surge of energy, and not a temporary (and unhealthy) 'sugar rush.' Research shows that our brains consume about 50% of all the glucose consumed by our body, and they need to consume more glucose when we're expending more mental energy.

Sugar, known as a 'simple carbohydrate', and even some 'processed carbohydrates', break down easily in the body and enter the bloodstream quickly, providing you with a quick surge of energy. Food such as vegetables and fruits are known as 'complex carbohydrates'; they break down and enter the blood stream slowly. You want to maintain your glucose levels, but in a *sustainable* way.

Everything you consume either helps, builds, or harms your body. Proteins build (and re-build) tissue. Carbohydrates provide energy. Fats store energy, insulate, and help absorb vitamins. Make sure you consume a healthy breakfast that sets you up for maximum productivity, eat balanced and controlled meal portions through your day to supplement your energy and concentration, and avoid unhealthy sugar consumption or excessive caffeine.

Eat right, day after day, and you'll start to see the difference in your physical and mental energy levels, and in turn, your ability to focus.

Focus Fuel Method 4: Kick off your day with exercise and energy

While exercising at any time of the day is beneficial, morning exercise can be the most potent for enhancing focus and mental energy. It helps you kick off your day right, and you don't have to struggle to make time for exercise in between a long day. It boosts your energy levels, helps shake off laziness and lethargy, improves your mood, and gets your mind running.

Here are a few great suggestions to start your day with a feeling of composure and more energy:

- Try stretching the first thing in the morning; it's not only a great way to wake up, but also warms up your body for any more rigorous subsequent exercise you may do.

- Release the strain in your back with a few iterations of yoga postures such as child's pose, cat pose, bridge pose or downward-facing dog pose. You'll find your entire body relaxed.

- Try doing squats. They're not excessively intensive and yet work on multiple areas of the body. Set up a workout including simple exercises such as planks, lunges, push-ups, jumping jacks or mountain climbers to get your body pumped up

Even just 20 minutes of morning exercise will help you better establish a daily routine, make you feel energized, put you in a positive mood, lower your blood pressure, and improve your sleep pattern.

Focus Fuel Method 5: Practice meditation to eliminate worry and anxiety

The last key component in your focus fuel arsenal is **meditation**. Meditation can be an extremely powerful practice which can boost your focus multi-fold and, at the same time, replace your worry habit with optimism.

Meditation encourages you to embrace *silence*, which is difficult to isolate in the rush of the day, and it encourages you to develop a deeper level of mindfulness.

With the help of studies backed by sophisticated brain-scanning equipment, researchers have proven that meditation brings about physical changes in the brain. It makes the brain *stronger* by improving the connections between the cells in the brain.

The brains of people who meditate are likely to be able to process information faster, concentrate for longer blocks of time, and recall memories at a faster rate. Some studies have even shown that regular meditation helps lower the sensitivity to pain. In addition, you can improve your heart rate, and create stronger cognitive and emotional capacities.

To meditate, you have to get your mind to slow down and become still. It forces you to be aware of the *now*, to shift your perspective and zoom out of your day-to-day problems. Think of it as an indulgence, which over time compounds into a channel for increased focus, while simultaneously helping you evolve into a much more composed, resilient and positive person.

You could thoroughly embrace any one of the techniques for focus fuel, but ideally you should try to integrate all five strategies for the highest impact on your level of energy, flow and concentration. As you've seen, each focus fuel method can amplify the other, and each of them will compound with consistent focus and practice.

Empower Your Deep Focus: Conclusion

Congrats! Now that you have made it to the end of Deep Focus, you have earned the clarity and perseverance to laser-focus your attention where it matters most. I know you'll succeed with streamlining your focus and flow to align with your **Big Goals**.

As you improve and leverage focus in time, you will notice incredible advancements in both productivity and the quality of your thoughts. Yes, focus is like medicine for your brain and can rewire your internal circuitry.

In this final chapter, here are some fun activities you can take part in that can enhance your focus as well as provide a relaxing emotional state, as well as strengthen your brain's cognitive function.

We mentioned exercise in this book as a method to sharpen focus, but several types of exercise include taking long walks, going for a bike ride, or just traveling out of town for the day and hiking up a mountain.

Physical exercise strengthens your brain and, if you add in social benefits, it increases blood flow and cell growth. This all adds to fuel for your brain that affects the quality of your focus and overall well-being.

But, you should also embrace the downtime by allowing your mind to de-focus. In fact, just doing nothing and sitting there gives you the rest to restock energy as the brain reenergizes. During your down time, do something creative such as coloring or drawing.

Learn to play some music or take up a language. I learned to speak Japanese after arriving in Japan over 25 years ago, and to this day, still study this and several other languages. It has definitely improved my cognitive function and confidence.

I encourage you to keep your brain active, schedule rest periods for your brain and body, and build better mental habits to sustain healthy long-term cognitive function.

Imagine where you will be in three, six and twelve months from now by cutting down distraction, building better habits and maintaining focus for longer periods of time. By improving everything by 1%, you can make a 300% leap in focus and happiness within one year.

As for my past college years, I managed to pass the course—barely—and my former teachers would be surprised to learn that the student who used to spend all his time staring out the window eventually learned how to focus time and talent to become a productive powerhouse...but only when I want to be. I still waste time, play games, watch Netflix, and scroll through Instagram and TikTok for the latest dance rave.

But when I'm focused on the work that matters, I'm all in. I focus on what I need to in order to get things done.

In know you can, too.

Continue to return to this book for guidance and strategy implementation. In the meantime, I will see you in the next book in this series, and remember this final quote by one of my favorite authors, Eckhart Tolle:

"Realize deeply that the present moment is all you ever have. Make the Now the primary focus of your life."

Until next time my friend—continue to stay great, and design the life that you want, one day at a time, one moment at a time.

SA

The Fearless Confidence Action Guide: 17 Action Plans for Overcoming Fear and Increasing Confidence

Scan the QR code to access your copy NOW

"It's very important that we re-learn the art of resting and relaxing. Not only does it help prevent the onset of many illnesses that develop through chronic tension and worrying; it allows us to clear our minds, focus, and find creative solutions to problems."

Thich Nhat Hanh

About Scott Allan

Scott Allan is a bestselling author who has a passion for teaching, building life skills, and inspiring others to take charge of their lives.

Scott's mission is to give people the strategies needed to design the life they want through choice.

He believes successful living is a series of small, consistent actions taken every day to build a thriving lifestyle with intentional purpose.

By taking the necessary steps and eliminating unwanted distractions that keep you stuck, you are free to focus on the essentials.

You can connect with Scott online at:

http://scottallaninternational.com/

For podcast bookings, interviews or speaking events, you can contact Scott Allan at: scottallan@scottallaninternational.com

More Books by Scott Allan

With Scott Allan International, the learning never ends. With a vast library of resources and tools to help you build your ultimate dream and the lifestyle you want, here are more titles to take you to a deeper level of training in the **Empower Your Success** series: With Scott Allan International, the learning never ends. With a vast library of resources and tools to help you build your ultimate dream and the lifestyle you want, here are more titles to take you to a deeper level of training in the **Empower Your Success** series:

www.ingramcontent.com/pod-product-compliance
Lightning Source LLC
Chambersburg PA
CBHW021447070526
44577CB00002B/294